CONTENTS

CW01507849

Men of 7th Battalion, Northumberland Fusiliers (T.F.), at summer camp shortly before the outbreak of war, 1914.

NORTHUMBERLAND AND TYNESIDE'S WAR

VOICES OF THE
FIRST WORLD WAR

Neil R. Storey & Fiona Kay

AMBERLEY

This book is dedicated to the memory of the men and women of Northumberland and Tyneside who 'did their bit' in the First World War and to all who carry the torch of Remembrance today.

First published 2017

Amberley Publishing
The Hill, Stroud
Gloucestershire, GL5 4EP

www. amberley-books.com

British Library Cataloguing in Publication Data. A catalogue record for this book is available from the
British Library.

ISBN 978 1 4456 6942 7 (print)
ISBN 978 1 4456 6943 4 (ebook)

Origination by Amberley Publishing.
Printed in the UK.

INTRODUCTION

Tyneside and Northumberland in the First World War is not a volume of straight history, nor is it a book of distant or lingering memories compiled from accounts by those who served or lived through the First World War looking back on it many years later; instead, as the *Voices of the First World War War* series implies, this book seeks, as far as possible, to tell the story of the people of this region in their own words through letters, memoirs, official reports, and newspaper and magazine accounts written at the time. The authentic 'voice' of the Geordie can also be found in the wealth of verse and songs they wrote and we have chosen some of the most poignant of them for this volume too.

Some of the Northern Cyclists while on patrol duty along the Northumberland coast, 1915.

And what accounts they are, for they reflect so much of the courage, stoicism, modesty and humour of true Northern lads from them joining up, to training and through the hell of war. No British city outside London raised more battalions of soldiers for Kitchener's Army than Newcastle. There were nineteen service battalions raised for the Northumberland Fusiliers between the years 1914–15, with all bar one of them raised in Newcastle. The exception was 17th (Service) Battalion (N.E.R. Pioneers) raised by the North Eastern Railway in Hull but it should not be forgotten that this battalion also included many men from Northumberland. The Northumberland Fusiliers had a remarkable fifty-two battalions during the First World War, twenty-nine of which served overseas. This made them the second largest line infantry regiment in the British Army, with only the eighty-eight battalions of the London Regiment to surpass them in greater number.

Among wor lads were the battalions of the 'Newcastle Commercials', Tyneside Scottish and Tyneside Irish, who faced the hurricane of machine-gun fire on the first day of the Somme in 1916 – no regiment lost more men than the Northumberland Fusiliers on that fateful day.

What is still more remarkable is the fact that just about every active service battalion in the British Army, and every branch of the Royal Navy and Royal Marines, could find at least a Geordie or two within its ranks at some point. Indeed, numerous English, Irish and Scottish regiments can all be found actively recruiting men from Tyneside and Northumberland to join their ranks during the First World War and some of them ended up with Tyneside companies of their own.

The soldiers of the North have a long history and reputation for being good fighting men, and their county regiment in 1914 was the embodiment of that spirit. The Northumberland Fusiliers finds its roots back in 1674 and was granted the seniority of the 5th Regiment of Foot in the British Army, a seniority they were always proud of. They richly earned and upheld the regiment's traditions and had nicknames such as the 'Fighting Fifth' and the 'Old and Bold'. In 1914 Lord Kitchener himself said of them, 'I have often had occasion to thank Heaven that I had the Northumberland Fusiliers at my back. Tell them from me that I have often relied upon the Northumberland Fusiliers in the past and I know that I may

Signallers and cycle scouts of 6th Battalion, Northumberland Fusiliers (T.F.), on manoeuvres, 1912.

need to do so in the future.' Lt-Gen. Sir Brian Horrocks did not mince words in his introduction to the history of the regiment in the *Famous Regiments* series when he wrote of Geordies from the Northern collieries 'whom I have always regarded as making the finest infantry in the world'.

In a book filled with the words of those who were there, we could not find a better way to conclude the introduction than with a quote. Francis Buckley, who had been commissioned into the 7th Battalion, Northumberland Fusiliers (T.F.), and saw action with them from the Somme until the Armistice, summed up the men of the North Country perfectly in his book *Q.6. A and Other Places*:

I have a great respect and admiration for the men of Northumberland. Especially those who come from the country towns and villages, the farm-lands and mines in the northern parts of the county. As soldiers they have gained a name the world over, of which it would be idle for me to talk. A cold climate and a fighting ancestry that goes back many hundreds of years have produced some marked qualities in the race of Northumbrians today. There are few of them that are not true to type and few that you would not care to have as comrades in a tight corner. Their stubborn courage and contempt for danger have been proved again and again. The worse the outlook the more cheerful they seem to become... But for stark grim courage under the most awful surroundings they stand second to none. There is a streak of ruthlessness too, in their dealings with the enemy; a legacy from the old Border wars with the Scots. They are ready, if need be, to take no prisoners. A hard and strong but very lovable race of men. Yes, I think all the world of the men of the North, although I am not blind to their faults. Taken as a whole no more handsome or manly set of men can be found in the British Isles.

Strapping lads of the Northumberland Royal Engineers (T.F.), stripped to the waist doing physical exercises at their summer camp, Ripon, 1909.

Mobilization of the Territorials. Men of 4th Battalion, Northumberland Fusiliers (T.F.), marching down Priestpopple, Hexham, 5 August 1914. (Newcastle Library)

He was not far wrong. We hope this book will add something original to the canon of works on the county of Northumberland, Tyneside, and its people both at home and fighting abroad in the First World War, and that the authentic voices of wor lads and lasses published herein will speak to you with the same resonance that they spoke to us as we researched and complied this book, and their stories leave with you the same legacy. They deserve to be remembered.

Quo Fata Vocant.

Neil Storey & Fiona Kay
Northumberland, 2017.

1

THE OUTBREAK OF WAR

The dark clouds of war had been drawing in for some time and after the assassination of Archduke Franz Ferdinand, heir to the Austro-Hungarian throne, on 28 June 1914, it was no longer a matter of 'if' there would be war but 'when'.

The industrial areas of northern Britain, especially those along the coast that were engaged in the construction of the mighty warships for the British Navy, were seen by both the Government and the War Office as areas that would need the protection of military forces if war was going to be announced, if for no other reason than to reassure the public. Serious concerns were already being expressed in the press and by the general population over invasion and spies of two types – those who were spying for their German masters and those who would rise up to sabotage and destroy utilities, bridges, railways and docks.

On Thursday 30 July 1914 the *Evening Chronicle* reported:

Considerable consternation has been caused in South Shields by military activities on the sea front and the movements of detachments of regular soldiers armed with rifles and ball cartridges, who took up a position at the Lawe, overlooking the entrance to the Tyne, created quite a sensation in the borough. The arrival of the soldiers who were drawn from the Northumberland Fusiliers at Newcastle was totally unexpected and the inhabitants of the town were naturally in a curious frame of mind as to the meaning of the operations. A party of 30 or 40 Northumberland Fusiliers having obtained the services of a police officer as guide, marched to the sea front carrying rifles and bayonets and they were afterwards reinforced by a detachment of Royal Garrison Artillery from Tynemouth Castle with a machine gun.

The men established their headquarters at the pilot house on the Lawe which overlooks Shields harbour and appeared to make arrangements for a few days stay. Sentries were posted and the oil tanks at the entrance to the Tyne on the south side were also similarly guarded.

At Jarrow the officers and men of the special service section of the Durham Fortress Royal Engineers were on duty at the Drill Hall after receiving orders from the War Office on Wednesday night. Lieut. J. B. Hall is in command. The captains of the vessels lying at Jarrow Slake received instructions this morning to remove their ships as a fleet of about 30 British war vessels were expected on the Tyne today.

A number of army men on leave in Newcastle were hastily summoned on Wednesday to join their regiments and this morning some twenty soldiers left the central station. There were also a number of Naval men who had received a similar summons and who left by the earliest possible train. Through trains carried large numbers of men travelling south to their respective quarters.

Movements of stores were also carried out from Newcastle this morning presumably for coast defence purposes and steps were reported to have been taken with regard to the special service section of the Territorials, who have joined for coast defence work. Several of the leading officials of the North Eastern Railway in Newcastle were called to their posts at a late hour on Wednesday night and were reported to have been busily occupied with arrangements till and early hour this morning.

The following day, Friday 31 July 1914, military activity intensified and the *Evening Chronicle* filled more columns with lively accounts of these developments:

Naturally the chief defences of Newcastle are coastal; yet under the present necessity for precautions the railway and road traffic on the chief lines of communication are under strict surveillance. On the railway lines east, south and west of the Central Station every train was pulled up and the patrol party there satisfied themselves that the train was such as the time sheet purported. On the High Level and Swing Bridges also a more or less vigilant 'sentry go' was maintained and no doubt any traffic foreign to what was the ordinary everyday traffic over these important approaches north and south would be detected.

These precautionary measures have aroused a tremendous public interest and some strange interpretations were placed upon the most ordinary military movements. Those inclined to make a mystery of the proceedings had some ground for mystification in view of the sudden change of guards. But the explanation tended to show how ready the authorities were to meet the emergency, and incidentally, how great that emergency was felt to be.

When orders were issued for these special defences of the Tyne and Newcastle, the East Yorks Regiment, to who the duty was allotted, were in camp in Conwy, Wales. They could not arrive before 12.30 midnight and to take up the duty from 6 o'clock on Thursday evening until this relief was available, the Grenadier Guards, to the number of 200 were hastily despatched from London. They returned by special train about 11 o'clock this morning, the majority of them having spent a quiet night at the barracks on Ponteland Road. The section that had been on duty during the night had commandeered the waiting rooms between platforms 9 and 10 as sleeping and kit quarters and the guard set up there gave rise to the story that the Central Station itself was under military control.

The Grenadier Guards were relieved by the East Yorks, who number 65, and who are quartering on the Swing Bridge central platform and at convenient points in the vicinity.

On the Town Moor, this morning, the Garrison Artillery were following their usual gun practice but under a keener realisation of the actual conditions under which their services might be required and the manoeuvres were watched by fairly large crowds.

Men of the Tyne Electrical Engineers at Clifford's Fort, North Shields, 1914. This unit was among the first to be at their posts on active duty on the eve of the outbreak of war, shining their searchlights out to sea on 31 July 1914.

The searchlights at Tynemouth were in operation up to midnight and a strict look-out was kept on all incoming vessels. Great excitement continued to prevail this morning at Tynemouth and North Shields but there appeared to be no new development and no further war vessels had reached the harbour up to noon. Activity had not slackened in the vicinity of Tynemouth Castle and the Spanish Battery, where the harbour defences were being carefully watched. The arrival in the town of Sherwood Foresters quickened the interest of the people of North Shields and gave rise to the wildest speculation. Anxiety had been awakened at the prospect of food stuffs becoming dearer should the present uneasiness have more serious developments. Large numbers of people visited the seaside in the forenoon but a heavy mist hung over the coast and very little could be seen seaward.

The seaboard between Tynemouth and Blyth this morning was being patrolled by small parties of the Northern Cyclists. They carried side arms. On the instructions of the Admiralty, the South Harbour at Blyth, it was stated, is to be cleared of ships in the event of berthage at the Middle Jetty being needed for the accommodation of war vessels. Several Cargo steamers left the dock during the morning for sea but it is not anticipated that the herring trade will be affected. Meanwhile the special service section of the Durham Fortress Royal Engineers (Territorials) who have been on duty at Jarrow Drill Hall since Wednesday night proceeded to South Shields this morning to take up duty at Frenchman's Bay.

Sgt Jack Dorgan recalled:

I was a member of the Special Section of B Company, 7th Battalion Northumberland Fusiliers, I was called up on the Thursday before the Declaration of War. I was in the fore-shift working down the Bothal Pit of the Ashington Group of collieries. No pit head baths in those days and after a meal and wash in front of the fire I was in bed, fast asleep in the afternoon when a policeman called at our house and told mother I was to put on my army uniform, with my rifle and ammunition etc. and report to the Drill Hall in Ashington.

At that time we had no idea of why we were being called, only a few days before we had had our fortnightly training camp at Scarborough and there had been no mention of any coming trouble or war except news in the newspapers of troubles in Ireland so after inspections and roll calls, we formed up outside the Ashington Drill Hall, set off and marched some 3 miles to Newbiggin by Sea where we were billeted in the various hotels in Newbiggin. The hotel I was allotted to were not very pleased to have us as it was Bank Holiday weekend and their visitors would perhaps have to be cancelled. However, we were installed, a number of us in a room used generally for meetings.

We were told by our officers that we were in Newbiggin to protect the cable station which had a cable going over to Norway. The cable station was on the sea front with Newbiggin's lovely sands down to the sea. We maintained a full 24 hour guard, patrolling up and down, rifle on shoulder, along a stretch of cement pathway about 24 yards in length. During the night watches we entertained the local Police Force, teaching them how to play cards for money and during the daylight hours, watched by the hordes of visitors from Newcastle asking us what it was all about, we soldiers felt very proud to be out on view, parading in front of all the children and grown-ups on holiday, maybe we thought we were in front of Buckingham Palace.

Over the weekend of 1 and 2 August the military presence remained in Newcastle, along the Tyne and on the coast. On a national level Sir Winston Churchill, the First Lord of the Admiralty, instigated the summons to all reservists for the full mobilisation of the fleet and the Admiralty order calling up all classes of naval reserves, which reached some towns as early as 4.00 a.m. on the morning of Sunday 2 August. Newspapers were able to report on 3 August that the Royal Fleet Reserve and Royal Naval Reserve had been called out, all preparations were complete, all the effective ships of the fleet were in a state of instant readiness and every seaman, marine or reserve, was at his post of duty.

Meanwhile, on the international stage, the situation on Monday 3 August was that Germany had requested that Belgium let its troops pass through, but Belgium had categorically refused and asked Britain to intervene and request an assurance that Belgian wishes would be respected. The request was sent and the world watched and waited for the response.

In England, Monday 3 August was a bank holiday and despite the main local railway companies cancelling their excursions in the light of the world crisis, most people made the best of it by visiting local beauty spots they knew and loved, like Jesmond Dene or the seaside resorts of Whitley Bay or Tynemouth. The *Newcastle Daily Journal* commented, 'For all the sunshine however, there was a cloud of which cognisance could not be lost, which there is little doubt made the holiday for many people, one scarcely to be remembered with gladness – the cloud of war. Wherever people congregated, the conflict on the continent was the chief topic of conversation and one naturally which could not be discussed without anxiety.'

On Tuesday 4 August Sir Edward Grey, the Secretary of Foreign Affairs (a descendant of the Earl Grey honoured on the great Newcastle monument and a figure well known to the people of Northumberland), wired to the British ambassador in Berlin asking for a reply from Germany before midnight.

Newcastle was set abuzz during the day when the posters went up announcing the mobilisation of the Army Reserve, and the majority of the 1,766 reservists of the Northumberland Fusiliers were soon seen making their way up Barrack Road to their depot. *The Journal* recorded: 'There was no mistaking these Reservists, for all their civilian attire. They had the upright carriage and swinging step that proclaimed the old soldier at once. Some of them were accompanied by their wives, many of them with young children clinging to their skirts, there was many a moving scene as the women dashed the tears from their eyes as they bade their "bonny lad" go and do his duty.'

At 11.00 p.m. the message came through to the telegraph and newspaper offices that war had been declared against Germany. Often the news was met with cheering in the streets as the population welcomed what they saw as the chance to 'take the upstart Germans down a peg or two', but others were not so ebullient. Bob Murdie, who went on to serve as a Territorial with 4th Battalion, Northumberland Fusiliers (T.F.), was at the Hexham Show when the news came through and recalled 'you never see such a change of faces in your life from pleasure to sour'.

The Regulars of 1st Battalion, Northumberland Fusiliers, were at Cambridge Barracks in Portsmouth in July 1914, as recalled by Brigadier H. R. Sandilands in *The Fifth in the Great War*:

Events in Europe had moved rapidly. With the increasing gravity of the situation, it seemed at long last a crisis had arisen that was destined to come to a head, instead of passing in the customary manner. But it was not, perhaps, till the declaration of a 'precautionary period' on 27 July that the full sense of the realities of the situation came to the Battalion ... In the 1st Battalion, waiting anxiously on events, tension was extreme. The few days that elapsed before the country's decision was made seemed endless. The time, however, was not spent in idleness. Though mobilisation had not been ordered, the situation was so acute that all preparations that could be made before the calling up of the Army Reserve were undertaken in anticipation of the order. So when, at last, at 6.00 p.m. on 4 August the order to mobilise was received the Battalion was well ahead of schedule. On the morning of 6 August the first draft of 420 men from the Reserve arrived from the Depot and a further draft of 221 reached Cambridge Barracks late the same night. As recently as the previous winter the annual Army Horse Census had been regarded by farmers and other horse owners as a pleasing farce and an Officer of the Fifth engaged on it had been subjected by them to much good-natured chaff when classifying horses for mobilization purposes. Yet, early on the morning of 7 August, the horses earmarked for the Fifth were no longer in their home stables in Berkshire but in the transport lines of Cambridge Barracks. Mobilization had been completed and on 9 August the battalion at full war strength paraded for inspection by Brigadier General Shaw.

The men of the Territorial battalions were mobilized to report for duty early on the morning of 5 August 1914. In the days before computers the orders to mobilize were sent by post to each individual soldier of the Territorial Force backed up by telegrams, telephone (if they had one) and a prearranged 'knock list' managed by the NCOs of their local platoons. To get some idea of the scale of the operation, remembering that each of these units would have consisted of between 800–1,000 men, what follows is a list of the Territorial Forces of Northumberland as published in *Kelly's Directory* 1914:

The Territorial and Reserve Forces of Newcastle & Northumberland:

Royal Naval Volunteer Reserve (Tyneside Division) HMS *Calliope*
Northumberland Fusiliers, 1st, 2nd and 3rd (Special Reserve) Battalions, The Barracks
Durham Light Infantry, 3rd and 4th (Special Reserve) Battalions, The Barracks

Territorial Force
Northumberland Hussars (Yeomanry), Northumberland Road, Newcastle:
A Squadron, Northumberland Road, Newcastle
B Squadron, South Shields
C Squadron, Morpeth
D Squadron, Hexham

1st Northumbrian Brigade, Royal Field Artillery, Barrack Road:
1st, 2nd and 3rd Northumberland Batteries
1st Northumbrian Ammunition Column

Tynemouth Royal Garrison Artillery (for Defended Ports), Drill Hall, Military Road, North Shields
No. 3 Company, Seaton Delaval
No. 4 Company, Sea View, Blyth

Northumbrian Divisional Engineers, Barras Bridge:
1st (The Newcastle) Northumbrian Field Company
2nd (The Newcastle) Northumbrian Field Company
Northumbrian (Newcastle) Divisional Signal Company
Tyne Electrical Engineers, Nos 1, 2, 3 and 4 Companies, Clifford's Fort, North Shields

Northumberland Infantry Brigade
Headquarters 6, Eldon Square
4th Battalion, Northumberland Fusiliers (T.F.), Battle Hill, Hexham
Companies:
A Company, Battle Hill, Hexham
B Company, Bellingham
C Company, Haydon Bridge
D Company, Prudhoe
E Company, Corbridge
D Company, Drill Hall, Haltwhistle
G Company, Newburn

5th Battalion, Northumberland Fusiliers (T.F.), Headquarters Drill Hall, Church Street, Walker
Companies:
A, B and C Drill Hall, Church Street, Walker
D, E and F, St George's Drill Hall, St Mary's Place, Newcastle

6th Battalion, Northumberland Fusiliers (T.F.), Headquarters, St George's Drill Hall, St Mary's Place, Newcastle
A-H Companies, St George's Drill Hall, St Mary's Place, Newcastle

7th Battalion, Northumberland Fusiliers (T.F.), Headquarters, Alnwick
A Company, Copper Chare, Morpeth
B Company, Drill Hall, Ashington
C Company, the Armoury, Wooler
D Company, Alnwick
E Company, Amble
F Company, Rothbury
G and H Companies, Ravensdowne, Berwick-Upon-Tweed.

Northern Cyclist Battalion, Drill Hall, Hutton Terrace, Newcastle.
Northumbrian Divisional Transport & Supply Column, Army Service Corps, St George's Hall, St Mary's Place, Newcastle.
Royal Army Medical Corps
1st Northumbrian Field Ambulance, Drill Hall, Hutton Terrace, Newcastle
1st Northern General Hospital, Drill Hall, Hutton Terrace
1st Northern Clearing Hospital, Drill Hall, Hutton Terrace

Mobilization card issued to Pte Thomas Cuthbertson 'in the event of emergency', March 1914.

From March 1914 every Territorial soldier had been issued with a mobilization checklist. Locally printed on card or paper for each unit, it clearly stated, in the event of mobilization, where and who the soldier should report to and outlined exactly what uniform he would be expected to wear, the kit he should be carrying and what he should ensure he was carrying in both equipment and his pockets when he reports for duty.

The Territorial Force embodiment notices had also been printed and had been waiting in the hands of adjutants for every battalion, ready for the word go. Stamped with their unit and date, all that had to be written on them was the soldier's name and the time he was to report. The adjutant signed it off and into the post it would go. Printed on the reverse was a confirmation of the uniform and equipment the soldier should bring and even a special request, like that printed on the reverse of the notices sent to men of the 6th (Newcastle) Battalion, Northumberland Fusiliers (T.F.): 'If you have a pair of field glasses, compass or a cyclists road map of the district, bring them with you.'

Once they had reported for duty, officers and men were medically examined and then two companies of the 6th Battalion were ordered to relieve the regular soldiers on guard at Central Station and other key locations of the city, while others were sent to prepare stores and transport and to arrange billets for the battalion. Five companies ended up in Tilley's Rooms on Market Street and one company went to Benwell. In fact, on the night of 5 August 1914 almost every available space in the city appeared to be taken up by Territorial soldiers of one corps or another and a number of churchyards provided safe enclosure grazing for military horses.

Trooper Frank Cunningham of 'A' Squadron, Northumberland Hussars, had served his apprenticeship with Armstrong Whitworth at the Elswick Works and had

Horses commandeered from farms at Wooler for war service, 1914.

joined the Hussars in 1909. He was away in Glasgow when war was declared and wrote home on 6 August 1914:

My Dear Mater,
I got to Newcastle at 11.00 p.m. last night and found the headquarters of 'A' Squadron had been shifted to Gosforth racecourse where I joined them about midnight. This is an ideal place for our purpose, plenty of good accommodation for men and horses. We are sleeping in beds and it is much like camp, only better. There is no definite news yet as to our future movements but we are likely to be here a week and it is said we may stay here all the time. We just have just got to wait and see.

Frank wrote again to his concerned mother on 11 August:

It is certain that they will not send us to the front except under such extreme necessity that even you would not wish me to stay. I cannot and shall not do any more volunteering and the absence of any necessity to do so is rather a comfort. If the original plan of putting me in the Navy had come off I should certainly be in the thick of it and if I were free, duty would point to my putting in for one of the commissions in the regulars ... Our only real chance of fighting is in the event of a raid on the East Coast, but there are rumours of our being sent to India or Egypt...

The Northumberland Hussars were sent away on active service in Flanders with the 7th Division in early October 1914. Frank was shot in the leg and through the body at the Battle of Loos in September 1915 and died of his wounds on 1 October, a few days short of being just one year in the field.

No. 3 Troop, A Squadron, Northumberland Hussars, at the bottom of Clayton Street West, leaving Newcastle for Gosforth, September 1914.

Fuelled by patriotism and a great sense of not wishing to miss out on a great adventure with friends, volunteer recruits for the army rolled in thick and fast. All Northumberland Fusilier Territorial battalions were up to capacity within days and applications had to be made by the local Territorial Association to form reserve battalions. One of those who had vivid memories of joining the Territorials in those early days of war in August 1914 was George Harbottle of Gosforth:

G.  R.

THE

Northumberland Hussars Yeomanry
(RESERVE REGIMENT)

Want a limited number of recruits who must be good horsemen.

Applicants may present themselves at Gosforth Park for the usual test, at 10 a.m. any morning except Sunday.

BY ORDER,

O.C., Depot.,   **D. L. SELBY-BIGGE,**
Northumberland Hussars,   Major.

GOD SAVE THE KING.

Recruiting advert for The Northumberland Hussars, 1914.

G.  R.

1st Northumbrian Brigade R.F.A.

RECRUITS

ARE Wanted Immediately for Foreign Service. There are Vacancies for Gunners, Drivers, Shoeing Smiths, Saddlers, and Wheelers.

Age, 19 to 35.   Must be medically fit.

Height :—Gunners, 5ft. 6in. and upwards. Drivers, 5ft. 3in. to 5ft. 6in.

Army Pay and Allowances.

Men who can ride preferred.

Intending Recruits should apply at the—

DRILL HALL, BARRACK ROAD
(Opposite Football Ground.)
or at GOSFORTH PARK.

GOD SAVE THE KING.

Recruiting advert for the 1st Northumbrian Brigade, Royal Field Artillery (T.F.), 1914.

On the Monday [3 August], our cricket match was cancelled and we sat around talking about the war. One of the team was an officer and had his call up papers with him. He suggested we chaps ought to join the 6th Battalion the 'City Battalion' so we went to join up but they told us thay had no authority to sign anybody on so we joined up the Wednesday at St George's Drill Hall, St Mary's Place. I was put through a quick medical, the MO said 'He's alright, put him in.' Other members of the cricket team soon followed too.

George joined A Company, 6th (Newcastle) Battalion, Northumberland Fusiliers (T.F.), and he recalled:

It was known as a 'Quayside Company' made up of commercial people and was always disliked by the rest of the battalion who came mainly from Wallsend and were shipyard workers and so on they thought the men of A Company were a bit 'up street.'

Shortly after being mobilized the 6th Battalion was billeted at the schools on Jubilee Road near Killingworth and then on to Newsham Road School, Blyth. Accommodation was basic to say the least and the men ended up sleeping on the hard floors while at the schools. Their training at this time was a mixture of squad drill, route marches, inspections and exercises. George remembered 'There was always a grumble from the others that A Company marched too fast but then we were fitter than the others.'

Initially the Territorial Force had sufficient uniforms to kit out the new recruits on enlistment but stocks soon began to run out. When Bob Murdie joined the 4th Battalion, Northumberland Fusiliers (T.F.), at Hexham Drill Hall in November 1914, he went through a strict medical examination before being passed fit. He began his

THE SPANISH CITY, MILITARY QUARTERS, WHITLEY BAY 338

The Spanish City, Whitley Bay, commandeered as military quarters for 5th Battalion, Northumberland Fusiliers (T.F.), while on coastal defence duties, 1914.

training at Hexham, then with the battalion at Dudley and Blyth, with regular visits to the rifle range at Ponteland. His battalion also had schools as billets, sleeping in blankets with his backpack as a pillow. He joked, 'You soon got used to it – you had to!' It was six weeks before he got his uniform.

When at Blyth, the 6th Battalion conducted exercises along the sand dunes and the men got to know the area only too well. In December 1914 the German fleet shelled Scarborough, Whitby and Hartlepool, George Harbottle recalled, in response to the bombardment: 'They immediately made us go and stand on those blasted sand dunes for two hours on and four hours off on a bitter winters' night that wasn't funny at all. To defend the area from a German attack, what the Dickens they thought any German attack would come there for? We just gazed out to sea. Mind you in Blyth there were some good positions. There was a squad on the lighthouse now that was the most comfortable place you could possibly imagine but the one in the Docks had millions of rats there.'

Kitchener's Army flexed the perimeters of age applied to those wishing to enlist both for those too young and those too old, especially if the man volunteering had previous military service. Among those proud to be back in uniform after many years was sixty-four-year-old Sgt Carmichael of Robert Street, Scotswood, who had served twelve years in the Royal Horse Artillery, which he had left in 1884, and was back in the king's uniform again in 1914 serving with the Royal Field Artillery.

Members of the Northern Cyclist Battalion (T.F.) who patrolled the Northumbrian coast during the invasion scares of the early months of the war and through the cold winter of 1914–15.

Right: One of the newly uniformed recruits for the Northumberland Fusiliers in his economy pattern jacket with no pleats and leather buttons, *c.* 1914–15.

Below: Soldiers of 6th Battalion, Northumberland Fusiliers, ready for inspection in front of their tent line at Gosforth Park, September 1916.

John Pickard of Alnwick was too young to enlist when war broke out in 1914. So when he encountered a pal going along to enlist on the street in April 1915, he thought he would go with him and try again. When he took his turn in front of the colour sergeant he was asked: 'How old are you?' Pickard replied 'I am nineteen the next birthday'. The sergeant accepted it, sent him up to the doctor and he was in. John would reminisce: 'They were not bothered, as long as you passed the doctor you were in. I joined on 14 April 1915 aged 15 and a half. Me mother didn't like it, me father said "You know what you've signed for? What's facing you?" I said "Yes I know exactly what I've signed for" and it was left at that.'

John enlisted into 7th Battalion, Northumberland Fusiliers (T.F.), and got his uniform issued straight away, sized by eye, at the Alnwick Drill Hall. The uniform was, he noted, of the economy pattern and the buttons made of leather rather than the smarter brass. His initial training was at Alnwick for the first ten days to two weeks. There he was taught to march, form fours and get used to taking orders. Then he and his draft were sent off to Newsham near Blyth where they were around twenty-two to a tent, sleeping on the grassy floor upon a groundsheet and three blankets. Every man had with him his kit bag, equipment and rifle – it was cramped to say the least. The feat was achieved by two to three getting into the tent first with all the blankets; they would make one bed all the way round, overlap the blankets then each man went in with his kit bag, crawled underneath the blankets and used the kit bag as his pillow.

Food was good at Newsham, John recalled:

Sometimes in the morning you would get eggs on toast, steak and onions, tripe, bacon, and on a Sunday instead of the cooks having to took tins of salmon and preserved foods would be dished out for breakfast and lunch. I was never really hungry. You could buy a cup of tea and a wad in the canteen in the evening too. If not on duty such as sentry guard you could pop down the local pub for a drink.

On learning how to shoot and of route marches he recalled:

First firing was with a .22 shooting at the back of a colliery tip where there was a 22 range 25 yards firing at a 6x6 inch target then when you eventually got to know what a rifle was, where the sights were and that sort of thing we used to go along to this big range at Whitley Bay, used to have machine guns and all sorts of things there but of course we were confined to the rifle.

We used to go along there every morning used to march from Newsham, Seaton Delaval way to Whitley Bay every morning. On Route marches the band was in front but all you would hear was the thump, thump, thump of the drum. We would march along singing parodies, rough ones up against the officer or the sergeant and they couldn't stop you. Officers would say 'stop that noise' but then somebody at the back would start again. All sorts of parodies, some we used to make up were:

'With me shirt on wire, I walked along the wire, with me little wiggle waggle in me hand.'
Or
'With me little bombing bucket in me hand,

I went up to the trenches.
With a big flare pistol, a compass and a map
They gave me six bombers and they chased me down a sap
I was shaking and quaking,
for by the block I knew I had to stand
When Fritz he came across he was fairly at a loss
When they saw the bombing buckets in our hands.'

Twelve men and one NCO to one bell tent was the usual for the 6th Battalion,
Northumberland Fusiliers, camp at Gosforth Park in 1914.

2

KITCHENER'S ARMY

On the outbreak of war national military hero Lord Kitchener was appointed Secretary of State for War. He was one of the few senior political or military figures who was far-sighted enough to see the war was not going to be over by Christmas; indeed, he was of the opinion it would take three years and seventy divisions to have a chance of winning the war. At the time there was no conscription in Britain (this was only introduced in January 1916). Kitchener wanted to expand the army but as a man who did not like to be bound by red tape or military bureaucracy, he sought a sanction from the war cabinet for an expansion of the British Army by 500,000 men, not for the Regular Army, not for the Territorials but "New" Armies that

Recruiting posters for the 'Commercials', c. 1914.

The Exchange, Quayside, Newcastle. It was from here and in the surrounding businesses and industries that many recruits for 'the Quaysiders' and 'the Commercials' answered the call in 1914.

Some of the men of B Company, 9th (Service) Battalion, Northumberland Fusiliers, 'the Quaysiders', dressed in their 'Kitchener Blue' uniforms, 1914. (Newcastle Library)

soon became known as 'Kitchener's Army', filled with ranks of volunteers proud to call themselves 'Kitchener Men'. Men from all backgrounds answered the posters that stated 'Your Country Needs YOU'. Some 1,100 men enlisted for Kitchener's Army in Newcastle in the first eleven days of the campaign and thus it is Newcastle that can proudly claim it raised the very first battalion of any English regiment in Kitchener's Army (registered complete on 21 August 1914). This unit became 8th (Service) Battalion, Northumberland Fusiliers.

From the earliest call for volunteers to 'do their bit', eclectic groups of friends, school old boys, sports teams and supporters, neighbours and work colleagues went along to join up together so they could train and serve together. In many areas of the north the units they raised became known as 'Pals' battalions. Although there were no battalions that bore that nickname in Northumberland, the bonds were just as strong in units that were raised, such as 'Quaysiders', 'Newcastle Commercials', Tyneside Scottish and the Tyneside Irish.

On 28 August it was announced the War Office had granted permission for the Newcastle and Gateshead Chamber of Commerce to raise a company of 250 men. The quota was reached in just a handful of days – many of the volunteers came from the offices, shops and businesses on the Quayside, hence these lads become known as and were very proud to be called 'Quaysiders'. What they lacked in military training they made up for in enthusiasm and in a few days they were given orders to proceed to their training camp outside Newcastle as the new B Company of 9th (Service) Battalion, Northumberland Fusiliers. How true their company song would prove to be:

> Just a company of penmen-
> Soldiers then, of little worth;
> But we set the ball a-rolling
> In the hard and fighting North.

A letter from Rutherford School old boy Pte Leonard Sanderson capturing life in those early days at training camp was published in *The Rutherfordian* in December 1914:

Tent A 7, B (Quayside) Co.,
9th Northumberland Fusiliers,
Bovington Camp,
Wool,
Dorset

Dear Sir, – Perhaps you would be interested to have an account of the Rutherford College Boys who have joined Kitchener's Army.

We enlisted on Thursday, the 3rd September, at the Grammar School, and were duly examined by the doctor and sworn in. There were several tricks practiced by to pass the doctor. Your chest measurement was taken with a shirt on, and an allowance was made. I know a man who was doubtful about his chest being 34 inches in circumference. He put on four undervests, and on his attestation form it had expanded to 36 inches. Several other dodges were employed, such as learning the eye test off by heart, and standing on tip-toes for the height, but the most impudent of them all was the trick practiced by a man who had another man go before the doctor for him, but, fortunately or unfortunately, this device was discovered.

On Saturday evening we were sworn in, and we proudly inflated our chests, for were we not, live soldiers of the King? We were then dismissed until Monday morning. On Monday morning we drilled until 12.15, when, to our great surprise, we were asked if we were prepared to go to Dorset at once. Of course we enthusiastically yelled, 'Ay, ay!' We were then told to parade at the Grammar School at 3 o'clock with food to last the journey, and were advised not to take good clothes, or any changes, towels, etc., as everything would be provided. On Monday evening at 10.30 p.m., after a great send-off, we entrained for Wool. The journey lasted fifteen hours, and we reached Wool about 2.15 p.m. on Tuesday after a very tedious ride. It was a very round-about way we came – we touched York, Sheffield, Derby, Burton, Birmingham, Cheltenham, Swindon, Andover, Salisbury (Twice) and Warham.

On arrival at the station we were marched up 3 miles to the camp where we were not expected until a week later. Consequently there were no tents or anything at all for us. Nevertheless our Quartermaster obtained two biscuits a man and some 'bully beef' but we had to sleep in the open with a blanket between two of us. That night I slept on a sheet of corrugated iron, which, to say the least, was slightly harder than a feather bed. During the night it rained a little but not much. Next day we pitched tents and began to settle down as soldiers. There are fifteen in a tent, which is rather a crowd, but in times like this it cannot be helped. About thirty men from the battalion (not in the Quayside Company) deserted. It rained all that week but we kept our spirits up by singing and working.

Our daily programme is as under:

5.30 a.m. Reveille – Turn out, shake blankets, roll up tent walls, clean windows, tidy up tent and kit.

6.00 a.m. – Gunfire, i.e. cups of tea with neither sugar not milk in it. The tea is vile but we have to endure it. If we were to see any milk, I should think we would faint. Wash and shave, brush up our clothes and make ourselves generally respectable.

6.30 a.m. – Parade. Double and march about 5 miles. This is really decent and very good for putting us into condition.

8.00 a.m. – Breakfast of tea (as above), bread, jam and a little bacon.

9.00 a.m. – Parade. Physical Drill till 12 o'clock

12.00–2.30 p.m. – Dinner of meat and *a* potato.

2.30–4.30 p.m. – Drill

5.00 p.m. – Tea of bread, jam and tea.

5.30–6.30 p.m. – Battalion Drill.

9.00 p.m. – Everyone to be in camp.

9.30 p.m. – Lights out.

You will see from the above that we are kept very busy but everyone is keen and is dying to have a smack at the enemy. We have no uniforms yet but live in hopes. Each of us received three shirts, one razor, a kit bag, a tooth brush, a hair brush and socks. Every Tuesday and Saturday we go for a 20-miles route march. Our officers are all good sorts and at present the officer commanding is Captain C. E. Grey, Viscount Howick, Earl Grey's son.

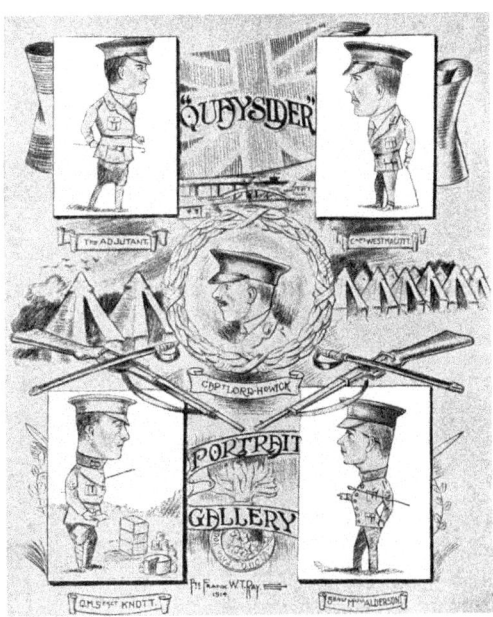

The officers and senior NCOs of 'the Quaysiders' drawn by one of the battalion's talented artists, Pte Frank Ray, 1914.

All leave is suspended and we are not allowed to leave camp. The food is rough but good. By the time we get home we shall have lost all idea of table etiquette. I think I have given you a general idea of what life in Kitchener's Army is like and if you take the rough with the smooth, it is all right.

Newcastle's most famous battalions of Kitchener's Army were the 'Newcastle Commercials', Tyneside Scottish and Tyneside Irish. The first of these three great units is raised by the Newcastle and Gateshead Chamber of Commerce. After the successful involvement in the raising of the 'Quayside' company when the government appealed for battalions to be raised by civilian effort for later adoption and refund of costs by the War Office, the chamber responded wholeheartedly and raised the first such battalion in the north in less than a week, registered and acknowledged by the War Office as such on 16 September 1914. These men became the 16th (Service) Battalion, Northumberland Fusiliers, known simply, with pride still felt in the town today, as 'the Newcastle Commercials'. The chamber also went on to raise the 1st and 2nd Battalions, the 'Tyneside Pioneers', which became the 18th and 19th (Service) Battalions, Northumberland Fusiliers (Pioneers).

Recruits of 14th (Service) Battalion, Northumberland Fusiliers. Only their officers and sergeant have their uniforms and a few Long Lee rifles have arrived to train with Halton Park Camp/ Buckinghamshire, 1914. (Gerry Embleton)

Recruits for the Northumberland Fusiliers in front of their barrack hut during training, 1915.

"SCOTLAND FOR EVER."

TYNESIDE SCOTTISH BRIGADE
"Harder than Hammers"

SCOTSMEN ON TYNESIDE

are given the opportunity to defend their Country's honour by

ENROLLING NOW

in this fine Brigade which is quickly being filled with the **Toughest, Hardest and Best Tyneside Fighting Men.**

AGE LIMIT 19 TO 45
HEIGHT, 5ft. 3ins. CHEST, 34ins.

Central Recruiting Office :

9 Grainger Street West, Newcastle
BRANCHES IN MOST TYNESIDE TOWNS

ONE MAN TO-DAY WORTH THREE IN THREE MONTHS.
GOD SAVE THE KING.

Andrew Reid & Company, Limited.

The famous recruiting poster for the Tyneside Scottish that bore the motto 'Harder than Hammers' for the first time, produced by Andrew Reid & Co. Ltd of Newcastle, 1914.

The Tyneside Scottish and Tyneside Irish both had rocky starts because of wrangles with the War Office that almost saw these great units lost before they really found their feet. The Tyneside Scottish suffered because the War Office was not prepared to grant permission for them to wear kilts. The Tyneside Irish Battalion offered to become part of the 16th (Irish) Division that was then being formed in southern Ireland. Their offer, however, was rebuffed by the division's commander Lt-Gen. L. W. Parsons, whose high-handed reply stated he wanted no 'slum birds' in his division, and on 20 September 1914 it was announced communication had been received from the Army Council that approval had not been granted for a Tyneside Irish Battalion to be formed.

Lord Kitchener was only too aware of the value of locally raised units and although the Tyneside Scottish had to accept they would only be granted Scottish headdress (only the pipers got to wear kilts and plaid), both Tyneside Scottish and Tyneside Irish got the go-ahead and rapidly went on to raise four battalions, no less than a brigade each before the end of 1914, 1st–4th Battalions, Tyneside Scottish, becoming 20th–23rd Battalions, and the Tyneside Irish 24th–27th Battalions, Northumberland Fusiliers.

One of the pipers of 20th (Service) Battalion, Northumberland Fusiliers (1st Battalion, Tyneside Scottish) wearing the distinctive Northumberland 'Shepherd's Plaid' tartan.

Mr Thomas Glass of Morpeth wrote the poem 'Tyneside Forever', first published in *Morpeth Herald* in February 1915. It was described as 'illustrative of the general appreciation of the lads of the north country who have donned the khaki in defence of the Country and Empire'. He captures the spirit of the times well:

> The Tyneside Scottish, with his tartan cap,
> His khaki jacket, what a fine looking chap,
> See him in the canteen, see him on parade,
> That's when he's hot stuff, 99 in the shade.

> Chorus –
> Northumberland,
> With men so grand
> Need fear no foreign foe.
> She may rest content,
> For these men are bent
> On putting the Hun below.

> The Tyneside Irish, with shamrock green,
> Is dying for a fight. O, the wild spalpeen,
> See him chewing barbed wire, see him in
> His lair.
> Oh, Willie, do be careful, say another prayer.

Chorus
The Tyneside Commercial, with his fine khaki suit
His long swinging stride in his number 9 boots,
See him on the Exchange, see him with his gun,
Now, Kaiser Willie, the war will soon be done.

Chorus

Above: Members of the Tyneside Scottish during their training in field signalling at Alnwick Camp, 1915.

Right: Advert for a 'Great Recruiting Meeting' for the Tyneside Irish in October 1914.

IRISHMEN, TO ARMS !

Great Recruiting Meeting

TYNESIDE IRISH BATTALION.

TOWN HALL, NEWCASTLE-ON-TYNE,
SATURDAY, OCT. 31st, 1914.

Speakers: THE RIGHT HON. THE EARL OF DONOUGHMORE,
T. P. O'CONNOR, Esq., M.P., and other prominent Speakers.

CHAIR WILL BE TAKEN BY

THE RIGHT HON. THE LORD MAYOR OF NEWCASTLE
(COUNCILLOR JOHNSTONE WALLACE)

At 5.30 p.m.   Doors Open at 4.30 p.m.

Music Programme and Organ Recital by N. H. Brown, Esq., F.C.O.

All Seats Free.   Enrol Now in Tyneside Irish Battalion.

GOD SAVE OUR KING AND COUNTRY.

The newly raised companies and battalions of Kitchener's Army used any available open spaces in Newcastle, be they parks, sports grounds or out on the Town Moor, for their initial training. Marching was a key element of turning the men into soldiers, for while doing so they learned discipline, working and bonding as a team and it got them fit. It was also great for recruitment, for these groups of friends and local men all going to do their bit would have pricked the conscience of many of those who preferred to stay at home. The saying 'come and join our happy throng' was repeated on many recruitment posters and notices and it was not unknown for single lads or groups of friends to tag along behind and return with them to enlist.

Joseph Keating wrote evocatively of the Tyneside Irish:

In their long route marches, sometimes twenty or thirty miles, they made a splendid picture – a column of five hundred or a thousand healthy, hardy, powerful-looking warriors in the making. Though it had not been possible as yet to find uniforms for all, the recruits had a magnificent appearance, whether in khaki or civilian clothes. Their faces had a cheerful, wholesome glow. Their bodies swayed easily to their trained, regular strides. They laughed and sang and their step rang out harmoniously – left, right, left, right. The huge column moved as one man. Through Newcastle and Gateshead Streets they marched along Tyneside or out into the open country of fields and fells... At different times their routes took them along the Tyne's northern and southern banks, away to the Shields. Sunderland, the Hartlepools, Durham, the Tees, in and around the colliery districts of Stanley, Dipton, Consett, Seaham Harbour, Horden, Easington and Thornley, and as the column of gallant recruits passed through their native places with a glorious swing, their eyes bright, their step well timed and their mood all gaiety in defiance of fatigue little children called out to them by name admiringly ... mothers, sweethearts or wives were among the groups of admiring spectators clustered at doorways, cheering the marching, laughing Irish lads as if they were the grandest sight in all the world.

Famously, the 1st Battalion, Tyneside Scottish, set off from Newcastle on 28 January 1915 to march the 40 miles (with an overnight stop in Morpeth) to their first purpose-built military camp at Alnwick. The weather was wet and foul for these lads but folks still came out to cheer them as they passed through their towns and villages.

The Territorials also had their recruiting marches. On Easter Tuesday 1915 150 men of the 7th Battalion, Northumberland Fusiliers (T.F.), stationed at Alnwick set out on a five-day recruitment march through north Northumberland under the command of Capt. Hodgkin. Arriving at Wooler, they received a great reception arranged by the local Red Cross ladies and the clergy. Staying there overnight, they were given a fine send-off and were each presented with a packet of chocolates by the ladies of Wooler for the next day's march through Chatton, Lowick, Ford and Crookham to Cornhill, then down the Tweed by way of Norham and Horncliffe to Berwick where they were played into the town by the pipers of the Royal Scots. Then on to Belford where they were well fed and stayed overnight before striding out to Bamburgh where Mrs Hart led the local ladies in the distribution of chocolates and cigarettes to all ranks, and then the men of the battalion set off on the final leg of their march back to Alnwick. In five days they covered 108 miles and only two men

Above: The Tyneside Scottish Brigade reviewed by Honorary Colonel the Duke of Northumberland K. G. on the pastures at Alnwick, 18 May 1915.

Below: The huts of the Tyneside Scottish (foreground) and Newcastle Commercials, Alnwick Camp, 1915.

ICK CAMP.

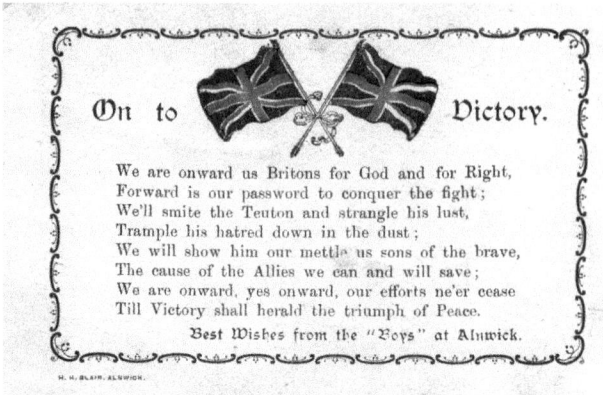

On to Victory.

We are onward us Britons for God and for Right,
Forward is our password to conquer the fight;
We'll smite the Teuton and strangle his lust,
Trample his hatred down in the dust;
We will show him our mettle us sons of the brave,
The cause of the Allies we can and will save;
We are onward, yes onward, our efforts ne'er cease
Till Victory shall herald the triumph of Peace.

Best Wishes from the "Boys" at Alnwick.

A fine greetings card with a patriotic message from 'the boys at Alnwick' produced by local printer H. H. Blair, 1915.

7th Battalion, Northumberland Fusiliers (T.F.) recruiting march at Wooler, 6 April 1915.

had fallen out. Special mention should be made of the battalion band of whom it was reported in the *St. George's Gazette* 'marched at our head the whole way and still had enough breath to play us through every inhabited part of the road'.

The Northumberland Fusiliers expanded from seven pre-war battalions to become the second largest infantry regiment in the British Army. There were nineteen service battalions raised for the regiment in 1914–15; all bar one of them was raised in Newcastle. Furthermore the level of recruitment achieved on Tyneside becomes truly phenomenal when you consider the significant numbers of volunteers that also came forward to join a host of other units in addition to their local Kitchener battalions by volunteering to serve with Regulars or Territorial Force units in both corps and infantry.

It is not surprising men in Northumberland also joined their neighbouring county's regiment, the Durham Light Infantry (DLI), and vice versa, men of Durham joined the Northumberland Fusiliers, especially when local battalions were completed and recruitment for them was closed, or the first incarnations of war-raised units such as the Tyneside Scottish or the Tyneside Irish were not accepted by the War Office, their volunteers looking for other local alternatives. The 9th Battalion, DLI, was a well-known local Territorial Force unit with its headquarters in Burt Terrace, Gateshead. Since before the war it did well with local recruiting, but the advent of Kitchener's Army saw the 10th, 11th, 12th, 13th, 14th and 15th (Service) Battalions of the DLI raised in Newcastle during August and September 1914. At the same time, men in the far north of Northumberland were drawn to the King's Own Scottish Borderers, and the 6th, 7th and 8th (Service) Battalions of the KOSB were raised in Berwick on Tweed, with many a man stepping forward in answer to the appeals for volunteers to join the Royal Scots Fusiliers and the Cameronians (Scottish Rifles) at the Morpeth Recruiting Office.

Far less well known is that in December 1914 an appeal was made directly to Newcastle for 250 men to raise a Tyneside company of the Inniskilling Fusiliers. The request for volunteers had come about because Northern Ireland was depleted of men of military age and it was open to all fit men regardless of Irish nationality or religion. Hundreds of local men, many of them of Northern Irish descent, joined under this appeal and as soon as they were sworn in they were despatched to Enniskillen Barracks in Ireland. The Inniskilling Fusiliers ended up with far more than a company's worth of Tynesiders in its ranks.

Having seen the success of the recruitment for the Inniskilling Fusiliers and having raised the four battalions of the Tyneside Brigade, the Tyneside Irish

Newspaper advert for the Morpeth Recruiting Office, 1914. Note the variety of regiments offered for immediate enlistment.

Band of 6th (Service) Battalion, Royal Inniskilling Fusiliers, 50th (Northumbrian) Division, 1918. When recruits became sparse in Ireland, direct appeals were made for recruits in Britain and many men from Newcastle answered the call.

Committee announced in January 1915 that they would forward new volunteers to Irish regiments so that 'Irishmen on Tyneside, who have missed the opportunity of serving with the local brigade, had a chance of drilling and eventually fighting, side by side, with patriots of the own kith and kin'. The regiments were: 6th Royal Irish Regiment, 7th Leinster Royal Canadians, 8th Royal Munster Fusiliers, 7th Royal Irish Rifles (Ulster Brigade).

Towards the end of 1914 recruitment began to tail off and the recruiting committees had to consider where they could draw more men from. Many a good volunteer had been turned away because he had not met the height criteria and so the War Office reduced the minimum height by 3 inches, and as a result, 'Bantam Battalions' were recruited. On 13 January 1915 the War Office gave permission for a Durham County Bantam Battalion to be raised with recruiting offices on Westgate Road, Newcastle, and on the High Street, Gateshead. Recruitment notices on posters and in newspapers stipulated the minimum and maximum heights for Bantam recruits was to be between 5 foot and 5 foot 3. The 5-foot man must have a normal chest of 33 inches; the 5-foot 1-inch man a chest of 33½ inches; and the 5-foot 2-inch man a chest of 34 inches. It was also required that each recruit must have a chest expansion of 2 inches, on top of normal measurements. The Durham Bantams became the 19th (Service) Battalion, Durham Light Infantry, and moved to Cocken Hall in May 1915 as a battalion of 1,000 men.

A Company, 18th (Service) Battalion, Northumberland Fusiliers (1st Tyneside Pioneers), 1915.

18th (Service) Battalion, Northumberland Fusiliers, at Ludgershall Station, Wiltshire, 1915.

Thousands lined the banks of the Tyne to watch the *Queen Mary* leaving Jarrow, Saturday 30 August 1913. She proved to be the last battlecruiser built by the Royal Navy before the outbreak of the First World War. She was sunk at the Battle of Jutland, 31 May 1916. (Newcastle Library)

3

THE WAR AT SEA

Tyneside and Northumberland men served with distinction in every major naval action in the First World War including the Battle of Jutland. Local sailors and people in general were also proud of the battleships and cruisers that had been built along the bank(s) of the Tyne, as the *Illustrated Chronicle* pointed out in 1914:

In the Home Fleets there are several notable Tyne-built vessels. The first Battle Squadron contains the *Hercules* of 20,000 tons displacement, built at Jarrow in 1911 and HMS *Superb* of 18,600 tons constructed at Elswick in 1907; while the First Battle cruiser squadron includes the *Queen Mary* of 27,000 tons, completed at Jarrow, delivered from Elswick in 1912, HMS *Monarch* figures in the Second Battle Squadron and HMS *Birmingham*, of 5,400 tons also sent out from Elswick, early in 1914 is among the First Light Cruiser Squadron.

The Royal Navy and its branches, Reserves and Royal Marine Light Infantry, also recruited well on Tyneside and Northumberland, notably providing considerable numbers of men for the Royal Naval Division (RND). This latter force was advertised in the *Illustrated Chronicle* in October 1914 as 'A Chance for Handy Men'. The accompanying article explained: 'When the European war broke out and all the naval reserves were called up it was found after manning all the ships and depots a good number of handymen were left for whom there did not seem any immediate opportunity of going afloat. Subsequently it was decided to establish a naval division for surplus reserves for field service abroad with Lord Kitchener's Army.' Prospective recruits were told to apply to Lt-Commander H. J. Craig (he was also MP for Tynemouth) at HMS *Calliope*, Elswick Works, Scotswood Road, or to HMS *Satellite*, Fish Quay, North Shields. Hundreds of local men responded to the appeal and were sent to the Crystal Palace Depot for training. No doubt aware that some recruits in Kitchener's Army had ended up sleeping on hard floors, the Naval Brigade recruiting adverts were keen to state that the men were 'immediately provided with hammocks and blankets and are kitted up within the first two days'. Standard requirement for enlistment was the candidate must be is 5 foot 3 inches in height with 34-inch mean chest measurement. Pay is 1*s* 3*d* per day, as well as separation allowance. It was also added that, 'Men with good eyesight and education will be recommended for the signal branch.'

G. R.

RECRUITS WANTED
FOR THE
ROYAL NAVAL BRIGADE.

Intended for Field Service Abroad.

ENLISTMENT for Period of the War. Pay and Separation Allowance, same as that now obtaining in the Royal Navy. Recruits must be under 30 years of age, minimum height 5 feet 4 inches; chest measurement 35 inches. After enrolment the Recruits will be drafted to the Naval Division depot at the Crystal Palace, London, where they will be trained and provided with proper equipment before joining one of the Naval Brigade Camps.

Application should be made on board, H.M.S. Calliope, Elswick Works, or H.M.S. Satellite, North Shields.

HERBERT J. CRAIG, Lt.Comdr., Commanding Officer.

A newspaper appeal for the men of the north to join the Royal Naval Brigade to fight on land in foreign theatres of war, 1914.

HMS *Amphion* encountered the German minelayer SMS *Königin Luise* while on patrol in the North Sea on 5 August 1914 and fired the first shells of the war at the enemy vessel. Private John Lindsay McCutcheon Brown-King, Royal Marine Light Infantry of Sheriff Hill, Gateshead, was the man who fired them.

Tynesider Fires the First Shot of the War

Northumberland's contribution to the war at sea during the First World War contains a notable first – the man who fired the first shot in action during the war. On 5 August 1914, the first full day of the war, the active-class scout cruiser HMS *Amphion* encountered the German minelayer SMS *Königin Luise* while on patrol in the North Sea between Harwich and the Dutch Island of Terschelling. Closing in on the German minelayer at around 11.15 a.m., *Amphion's* guns began to hit their mark and by noon *Königin Luise* was sinking. The following day *Amphion* was returning on a course where the captain believed he would be avoiding the mines laid by *Königin Luise*. Sadly he got it wrong. *Amphion* struck a mine, which broke her keel causing her magazine to explode and she sank in around fifteen minutes.

Among those rescued was Pte John Lindsay McCutcheon Brown-King of the Royal Marine Light Infantry. A well-known native of Sheriff Hill, Gateshead, he was the fourth son of Mr and Mrs Brown-King resident at No. 148, Esk Street, Windy Nook. Shipped to Shotley Naval Hospital as a result of the injuries he had received when *Amphion* blew up, the young man related his experiences to his parents while lying in a critical condition for three weeks.

He held the position of gun layer on the *Amphion* and told his parents, Frederick and Jane, that it was he who had the honour of firing the first shot and had the further distinction of shattering the German flag when the *Amphion* succeeded in sinking the *Königin Luise*. When the *Amphion* struck a mine the following day, Pte Brown-King escaped injury when the first explosion took place, but seeing one of his comrades enveloped in flames, he hastened to save him and it was when in the act of performing this heroic deed that he received mortal injuries in the second explosion. Pte Brown-King died of his injuries on 23 August 1914 and is buried in St Mary's churchyard, Shotley, Suffolk. He was twenty-three.

Fisherman Heroes

Merchant vessels suffered heavily from attacks from enemy U-boats and sea mines too but it is not generally realised that fishing vessels also came under attack. Censorship restricted the publication of merchant shipping and fishing boat losses, which was hardly surprising as the losses off our coast on a single day were shocking at times. Even the family announcements of the deaths of fisherman and relatives lost at sea were frequently censored out of the death notices in local papers. Often all that could be gleaned came from very short and unspecific weekly announcements such as: 'Two British vessels were sunk or captured during the week ending August 11th and 17 British fishing vessels were unaccounted for' buried in the side column of a page of war news. Although the loss of a fishing boat taken in isolation in the big scheme of the war could be viewed as 'insignificant', cumulatively the losses in British coastal waters were horrific and the impact on their families and fishing communities was profound.

The Fish Quay, North Shields, one of the main harbours for the herring fishing fleet that followed the 'silver darlings' around the coast of Britain, *c.* 1914. By the early twentieth century as many as 30,000 vessels were involved in herring fishing off the east coast alone. The zenith of the industry was in the years immediately before the First World War. During the herring boom of 1907, 2.5 million barrels of fish (250,000 tons) were cured and exported, the main markets at the time being north Germany, Eastern Europe and Russia.

North and South Shields were two of the ports where the herring fishing fleet would call every year as they followed the shoals of 'the silver darlings' around the British coast. The season had been a good one in the north east but the boats were noticeably fewer in number; the wartime waters were known to be infested with minefields. There had been losses since August 1914 and numerous fishing vessels had been taken over and refitted as minesweepers.

Crew members of fishing, trading and minesweeping vessels destroyed after contact with mines were landed at Tyneside ports. The ten survivors of the Hull trawler *Imperialist* were one of the few accounts published in some detail in the local press. She had been en route from Iceland bound for Hull when she stuck a mine 40 nm off Tynemouth on 6 September 1914. The skipper Joseph Wood and spare hand Thomas Jackson sadly drowned but ten of the crew had managed to scramble into a small boat and, after rowing all night, they were picked up by the steam fishing boat *Rhodesia* and landed at North Shields on the afternoon of 7 September. Battered, bruised and bedraggled, their 'pitiful plight' drew the sympathy of all and the question was raised: should fishing be stopped in the North Sea for the duration of the war?

Fishing was not stopped and with help from the minesweepers the brave fishermen dared to carry on to help keep Britain fed. The story of the *Lily* tells a tragic tale typical of so many fishing boats that were sunk during the First World War. The steam drifter of North Shields had just shot her nets when she struck a mine on Wednesday 7 October 1914. Nearby fishing boats *Fioandi* and *Oakland* came to her aid. *Fioandi* recovered the body of fisherman Frank Self (sixty-four) while Harry Blowers, the plucky skipper of the *Oakland*, rescued three survivors, Messrs. Dunham, Shillings and Nichols. Shillings and Nichols were suffering from minor injuries and shock but Daniel Dunham had been seriously hurt. He had been in his bunk filling his pipe at the time the boat struck the mine and was blown clean through the deck. The *Fioandi* and *Oakland* put into the Tyne by the evening and landed the survivors, who were taken to Tynemouth Victoria Jubilee Infirmary.

Among the seven members of the crew lost on the *Lily* were helmsman George Robert Chester Cockell, who left a wife with one child and within weeks of the birth of a second. Mrs Blake was prostrated with grief at the loss of her son William and tearfully remarked that his father, who was on board one of the lightships, did not know his son had gone to sea. It had been his first trip to sea and he had only recently written to his mother to say he had 'got with a very good crew' and was then 'quite safe'. Mrs Leonard, the widow of the third victim, was left with four little children.

The funeral service for Frank Self was held in the Mission for Deep Sea Fishermen at the New Quay. Some difficulty had been experienced in tracing the relatives of Mr Self, who came from Lowestoft in Suffolk, and there were none present at his funeral. However, in the true comradeship of those lost at sea, the funeral was attended by many members of the local fishing community including over 130 fishermen who escorted the coffin to Preston Cemetery, North Shields. A tragic postscript to the story was that brave skipper Blowers, who rescued the three survivors, had a number of his own crew leave him after they saw what befell the *Lily*. He had to bring his boat home short-handed, though he was not a well man himself. Despite being attended by a doctor, he died on 20 October, just a few days after his return, leaving a wife and three young children under five.

A German propaganda card for the sinking of the *Hogue, Cressy* and *Aboukir* by the *U9* on 22 September 1914.

Hogue, Cressy and Aboukir

A terrible blow was dealt to the Royal Navy when the armoured cruisers *Aboukir*, *Hogue* and *Cressy*, which had been engaged keeping North Sea waters south of Dogger Bank clear of German torpedo craft and minelayers, were all sunk by the German submarine *U9* under the command of Kapitänleutnant Otto Weddigen on Tuesday 22 September 1914. The crews of the cruisers had been made up with numerous Royal Navy reservists who had been called back to service in early August 1914. Many of them were older men in their late twenties and thirties who had left the Royal Navy to get married and start families and had left toddlers and young children back home. Many were well known among the fisherfolk and other sections of the townspeople and it was remarked on how a tension hung over the communities that nestled along the coast and the Tyne as the news of survivors or those who had been killed or posted missing reached their relatives by official telegram. In some cases wives and other friends received their telegrams on Tuesday night, announcing the safety of individual men and later news was received of others, but the uncertainty as to the well-being of others and the suspense of waiting generally cast a gloom over the towns during the whole week. Most affecting was the sight of the womenfolk's anxious calls at the Custom House, who hoped for information.

News of the fate of local sailors trickled back and was published in the local press. John Renwick, of No. 199 Albion Row, Byker, a gunner on HMS *Cressy* at the time the cruiser was sunk, was one of four who hung on to a capstan bar. Mr Renwick was rescued after four hours in the water, but his companions had all gone under.

Frederick Monks, artificer-engineer, was on board HMS *Cressy*. He had served in the Navy for nineteen years, a native of Wallsend, the youngest son of the late Thomas and Catherine Monks and brother of Mrs F. Murphy, Percy Gardens, Tynemouth, and had served his apprenticeship with Messrs Wigham Richardson. Monks had been picked up after being in the sea for four hours but died from exposure shortly afterwards. He was interred at Shotley with full Naval honours. The king and queen sent a message of condolence to his mother.

For many all they could do was wait to see if a telegram with news would arrive, and some would reach out for news via the local press, such as the *North Mail*:

William Burdis, of 13 Chaytor Street, Jarrow, who was on H.M.S. *Aboukir*, is amongst the missing. No news has yet been received concerning Walter Murray, of 26, Union Street, Jarrow, who was on H.M.S. *Cressy*. Both men are stokers and reservists. Murray was a shipyard driller, and Burdis was employed as a labourer at Palmers Shipyard.

News reached North Shields, yesterday, to the effect that Mr. J. J. Cheyne, who was engaged on board the *Aboukir*, is now at Amsterdam and quite well.

No word has yet come to hand about John Gibson, a stoker on board the *Hogue*, who lives in Hedley Street, South Shields, and there is also an absence of news in the case of John Hamilton, also a stoker on the *Hogue*, who resides in Palmerson Street, South Shields.

Another Shields man engaged on the *Hogue* as an engine room artificer was Mr. Craig Alexander, of Regent Street, South Shields. The relatives yesterday morning received a telegram from the Admiralty intimating that Mr. Alexander was saved, and Mrs. Alexander also received a wire from her husband from Ymuiden to the same effect.

Much anxiety is felt for the safety of two North Shields men named Jennings and Loft, who were stokers on H.M.S. *Hogue*.

Anxiety is also felt in Sunderland as to the safety of three men who are stated to have been on two of the ill-fated cruisers. Samuel Dick, a pensioned reservist, who had retired with the rank of Quartermaster, and who had 35 years' service in the Navy, joined the Hogue in August. A stoker mechanic named George Michael Slater, of 97, Dame Dorothy Street, was also on the *Hogue*. William Henry Corben, of 48, Hastings Street, Hendon, a naval reservist, was in the *Cressy*. Nothing has been heard of any of the three since the sinking of the cruisers.

It would be late September and early October before survivors of the sunk cruisers made it back home to Tyneside. One of the earliest first-hand accounts appeared in the *North Mail* on 5 October 1914:

Saved from HMS Aboukir when she was torpedoed on 22 September. Mr. J. F. Dry is on brief furlough and back home. A seaman torpedoman of the Royal Naval Reserve, he was called up at the outbreak of war. When disaster struck the *Aboukir* Dry's first impression was that an explosion had occurred on board but hastily realising the true position he went below and dressed and when the *Aboukir* turned turtle he jumped clear. He was in the water an hour

One of thousands of local lads who served in the Royal Navy and all its branches during the First World War. This young able seaman, a member of the Tyne Division Royal Naval Volunteer Reserve, was mobilized in 1914 and photographed at Elliots studios of North and South Shields while on home leave after *Triumph* was torpedoed and sunk off Gaba Tepe during the Dardanelles campaign by the German submarine *U-21* on 25 May 1915.

before being fortunate enough to secure a chair, he subsequently spent three hours on a raft with about 30 others, two of whom died and the sights he witnessed he declares were beyond description. Mr Dry's watch stopped at 6.55 a.m. and it was about 11 o'clock when he was picked up by the *Flora*. Landed at Ymuiden, Holland they were sent to a camp about 13 miles away from Balk. Fears of being interned there during the war were early dispelled and the party reached Sheerness a week ago and then proceeded to Chatham Barracks. Dry commented "My experience will not be readily forgotten but I feel little the worse and am returning to duty on Wednesday. I hope to get another boat and do my little in avenging our ill luck of 22 September."

A native of Hornsea, where his widowed mother resides, Mr Dry has been postman at Dudley and Seaton Burn for a number of years.

Approximately 1,450 sailors were lost with the sinking of the cruisers *Aboukir*, *Cressy* and *Hogue*.

The Tragedy of HMS *Viknor*

The first recorded loss of a British merchant vessel off the British coast during the First World War occurred on 5 September 1914 when the steamer *Runo* struck a mine 22 miles off the Tyne with the loss of twenty-nine crew and passengers. But the first major loss of life aboard a merchant vessel involving a significant number of men from the north-east was when the armed merchant cruiser HMS *Viknor* sank off the north-west coast of Ireland without sending a distress signal on 13 January 1915. Requisitioned by the British Admiralty service on the outbreak of war in 1914, the *Viknor* was outdated, slow and only minimally armed. *Viknor* was never expected to enter into combat with enemy warships; its role was to patrol between Iceland and Northern Scotland to intercept neutral shipping, board and inspect it for any war contraband destined for Germany. Her crew was a mixture of Mercantile Marine Reserve, Royal Navy, Royal Naval Volunteers Reserve, Royal Marine Light Infantry and Newfoundland Royal Naval Reserve.

The first indication the ship had been lost came when radio communication stopped, then when some of bodies of drowned crewmen began to be washed up along the Ulster coast, the worst had to be assumed. The *Viknor* had completed her articles at South Shields Mercantile Marine Office on 22 December 1914 and the majority of the men serving on the ill-fated vessel had been local men. The *Illustrated Chronicle* recorded:

Painful scenes were witnessed at the Mill Dam, South Shields, where the head offices of the Mercantile Marine Department were situated. A large number of relatives of men who were on board the vessel called to make enquiries respecting the announcement made in the daily papers yesterday morning. The officials were not in a position to give them any news of the vessel apart from that which had already been published and they wired to the Admiralty to ascertain whether there was any further information available.

The Admiralty, in reply, stated definitely that all hands were lost and that there was 'nothing to add to what had already appeared in the daily press'.

The announcements were made in the newspapers naming the crew of the *Viknor* with the dreaded words 'All hands lost'. The homes where their families lived drew their curtains and widows went into mourning black. Forty of the crew were from South Shields, and many of them were married men with children; some of them were from further afield but the majority of the crew hailed from the communities of Wallsend, North Shields, Pelaw, Jarrow and Gosforth.

Among those lost were such tragic cases as that of twenty-seven-year-old Sub-Lt Frederick Monks, son of Mr and Mrs John Monks of Park Road, Wallsend, who had joined the Navy at the start of the war can be found. His uncle, artificer-engineer Frederick R. Monks, lost his life at the sinking of HMS *Cressy*. Another was Lt William C. M. Johnson, also twenty-seven. He had served his apprenticeship with Newcastle shipping companies and qualified for his master's certificate at twenty-three and served aboard the *Viknor* in its previous life as the *Viking*, when it was used as a tourist passenger vessel. After war broke out, Mr Johnson took a desk job on shore for a while but when the Viking Cruising Co. asked him to take up the position of master after the *Viknor* had been acquired by the Admiralty, he leapt at the chance. He left a widow and a two-and-a-half-year-old son residing at Lish Avenue, Whitley Bay.

All next of kin of the 292 lost crew received letters of sympathy from the Imperial Merchant Service Guild. Most of the bodies were never recovered. Whether it was foul weather, enemy torpedo or from striking a mine, to date the exact cause for the sinking of the *Viknor* has never been ascertained.

Men of the Tyneside Division of the Royal Naval Volunteer Reserve and other internees at Groningen Camp, Holland. Our lads had been serving as fighting men on land in the First Royal Naval Division who retreated from Antwerp and crossed into neutral Dutch territory to become internees rather than be taken as prisoners of war by the enemy in October 1914.

Some of the Chinese stokers of North Shields.

Remember the Oft Forgotten

Almost as long as there have been steamships there has been a preference to employ crews from countries with hot climates because the crew members recruited from those countries were used to heat and were ideally suited to the extreme temperatures of working in engine rooms as firemen and stokers. During the later years of the First World War, with so many men gone to serve in the fighting forces, the local skippers expanded on their pre-war recruitment of those from hot climates and the trading and fishing vessels of the north-east became the most ethnically diverse they have ever been. International ships brought crews from all over the world, such as Lascars from the Indian subcontinent. Others came from Africa, a small community of Yemeni seamen was established in South Shields and small a community of Chinese crewmen lived in North Shields. Indeed, crewmen from countries as diverse as Finland, Sweden, Norway, Iceland, Holland, Greece and Malta can be found employed in all manner of work on ships sailing out of the north-east during the First World War. A significant number of those vessels, large and small, also went down with all hands as a result of enemy action and the names of crewmen from all over the world appear on the Tower Hill Memorial, London, which commemorates the dead of the Merchant Navy and Fishing Fleets who have no known grave.

The U-Boat War

A typical attack from a U-boat against a fishing or merchant vessel would often be preceded by the U-boat surfacing. The commander would appear in the conning tower and hail the crew of the vessel with a megaphone, and they would be given a five-minute warning to abandon ship before the U-boat would open fire upon the boat and sink it. If the ship had no lifeboats, the crewmen would simply be left in the water; some may be caught in the hail of fire, or they may even be taken aboard the U-boat and taken back to Germany to become prisoners of war.

An account published in the *Illustrated Chronicle* on 28 November 1914 is an absolutely typical scenario of challenge and subsequent destruction that was to be repeated throughout the U-boat campaign:

On arriving at his home in South Shields, yesterday, William P. Nelson, a seaman on board the Newcastle Steamer *Primo*, gave an interesting account of the attack upon the vessel by a German submarine. He stated that the Primo sailed from the Tyne with a cargo of coal for Rouen, and two days later, while the vessel was off Cape Antiger in the English Channel, he was about to go on deck to take charge of the wheel at 7.45 in the morning when one of his shipmates came into the forecastle and informed him that there was a submarine on the starboard side of the ship.

Nelson went on deck and saw a submarine lying to the starboard, but at that time he thought it was a British vessel. There were about eight men on the coning tower, including an officer, who, in good English, asked Capt. Whincop, the master of the *Primo*, whether his ship was British. The master informed the officer that it was, and in reply to a further question, he stated that the vessel was bound for Rouen with gas coal for the Paris Gas Company. Nelson observed some ribbons on the officer's cap and this convinced him that it was not a British submarine.

His suspicions were confirmed when the officer suddenly produced a German flag and informed Capt. Whincop that his crew would be allowed exactly five minutes in which to leave the vessel. The captain pointed out that his ship was a peaceful trader carrying no munitions or contraband of war, but the German officer replied: 'But you are British, and my orders are to sink you. War is war. There may be British or French cruisers about'. As there was nothing else to be done, the crew at once made preparations to leave the vessel, the Germans in the meantime pointing a gun at the steamer, apparently as a reminder that their instructions were to be obeyed.

The donkeyman and another member of the crew of the *Primo*, who were in their bunks, had just time to put on their outer garments and hurry on deck, while one of the engineers, who was on duty, was brought straight out of the engine room. The two lifeboats were launched, and 11 of the crew took their places in one of the boats, and seven in the other. Capt. Whincop being the last to leave the ship. The sea was very rough, and the boats were headed for the land, six miles distant. When they had gone about quarter of a mile, the submarine fired at the steamer, which was struck on the bows below the water line. The vessel did not sink, however, and the Germans fired again. Dense clouds of smoke were then observed coming from the funnel, the steamer having been struck amidships near the engine room.

The *Primo*'s crew were eventually picked up by a Grangemouth steamer and transferred to a pilot cutter, which landed them at Fecamp. When they last saw the Primo she was still afloat. Nelson stated that while the German submarine officer was conversing with the master of the *Primo*, the steamer *Spero*, owned by the same firm, and bound for the same destination, steamed past apparently unnoticed.

Merchant shipping suffered its greatest losses (by tonnage) during the unrestricted U-boat campaign of 1917. Most of the vessels off our coast in the cold North Sea were lost in offensive actions by the U-boats of the Flandern Flotilla, a formidable force during the war that was responsible for the destruction of no less than 2,554 merchant vessels (or around 4.5 million BRT), plus damage and destruction of numerous fighting vessels of the Royal Navy.

British fishermen in a German prisoner of war camp, 1917.

4

FROM FLANDERS FIELDS TO HELL ON THE SOMME

It seems that in almost every battalion in the British Army in every significant action, be they corps or infantry, you could find a Geordie, Tynesider or Northumbrian, and they can proudly say they were truly in the thick of it from start to finish. One of the major opening actions of the First World War was the Battle of Le Cateau, fought on 26 August 1914, just a handful of days after the British Expeditionary Force had first landed in France. Gunner Thomas Trobe of the Royal Field Artillery was present at the action and, remaining high in spirits, wrote home to his mother in Alnwick:

I am writing this in my little dug out on the hillside, the firing is quieter today…Le Cateau was a desperate affair. We were so outnumbered that each of our batteries had at least two of the enemy's batteries shooting at it. Our battery was very fortunate. We were posted behind a crest and the enemy could not locate us. We fired over 1,000 rounds of lyddite and shrapnel slap bang into them, simply mowing them down. It is safe to say if our army lost one man theirs lost at least six.

Sadly the opening battles, although fought valiantly, were not successful. September 1914 saw the British Army make their stand after their retreat from Mons with the battles of the Marne and the Aisne. Bedlington soldier Pte John Welsh was there with the 1st Battalion, Northumberland Fusiliers, and told of his experiences in a letter to his wife from his hospital bed in Glasgow after he was returned wounded:

I was in the big battle at Mons and at Inche and never got a scratch. I was wounded in the battle that is going on now, the Battle of the Aisne and I will never forget it. I was hit three times in the legs and I said to myself 'Come on you dogs. If I have got to die I will die with the rifle, I hope.' Blazing away with them, I ran short of cartridges but I got some out of a dead man's pouch beside me. The man belonged to Byker, Private Alexander poor lad! He always stuck to me in the firing line and trenches. Five hours after I received other shrapnel wounds. I was bleeding fast then. The yells of the wounded Germans were like pigs going to the hammer. It was turning dark and I started to pull myself away with my jack knife. I saw something moving towards me and saw it was a wounded German. He was wounded through the head and arms. He was moving faster than I was. I pulled myself behind a bush and when he put his hand on the tree I put my jack knife through it. That is the way I got shot of the German and I was pleased too. I crawled three miles to safety.

The First Northumberland VC in the Great War

Ovingham-born Pte Frederick William Dobson had originally enlisted into the Coldstream Guards in 1906 and had left the Army in 1909. He married in 1911 and by 1914 had made a home with his wife Rebecca in Meadowell, North Shields. Dobson remained on the Army Reserve and was recalled to the colours in 1914. Joining the 2nd Battalion, Coldstream Guards, he was in action at Chavanne on the Aisne on 28 September when he volunteered to go out under heavy fire not just once but twice to bring in two wounded comrades.

With the modesty that typifies all highly decorated soldiers, he was not given to talking too much about the deed himself, as shown in the letter he wrote to his wife shortly after the action:

It is with the greatest pleasure that I write this letter as it is our wedding anniversary – September 30. I only hope we shall spend the next one together. You will know by the time you receive this letter that I have been recommended for the VC. An honour I never thought would come my way. In fact, I do not yet realise that it is possible. I only took my chance, and did my duty to save my comrades. It was really nothing, but I shall never forget the congratulations and praise I received from our officers, my comrades, and our Brigadier-General.

Three of my comrades were out on patrol, when they were fired on by Germans. One got back to the trenches, though I was told two had returned. One I saw was wounded. I volunteered to save him. I went out, and was heavily fired at, but I had made up my mind to get to him, and you know I very seldom change that.

Well, I persevered, and got to one who was past human aid. I had missed the wounded one, who was lying nearer to the trenches. I came to the trench, and reported one. I went out again to the wounded man, and, with the help of Corporal Brown, brought him safely back. Corporal Brown was brave, and never showed the least fear. Well, this was all that happened.'

Pte Dobson was recommended for and received our nation's highest gallantry award, the Victoria Cross, for his supreme acts of bravery and was decorated personally by George V at Buckingham Palace on 3 February 1915. On his return to his native county later that same month he was given a civic reception in North Shields, was entertained for dinner by the Mayor of Tynemouth and was presented with a purse

Local hero Cpl Frederick Dobson VC seated centre and Pte Alfred H. Thomas DCM, *Medaille Militaire*, seated right, both of the Coldstream Guards pictured after a fine valedictory gathering, 1915. (Fusiliers Museum of Northumberland)

of gold raised by local subscription and given a hero's send-off by the people of North Shields when he left from the station for the front again.

As the days of war rolled on, the fighting intensified and the British Expeditionary Force was facing ever-increasing numbers of enemy troops. Pte William Underwood of Queens Road, Jarrow, was serving with 1st Battalion, Northumberland Fusiliers, when he was wounded during the First Battle of Ypres in November 1914. He wrote of the fighting:

One night we got orders to prepare for a charge after we had been making two charges each day for a week. We were opposed to the Prussian Guards, and we were ordered to take their trenches. I was fighting with a man about six feet, two inches in height, and I only had one shot in my rifle. I fired at him, and then used my bayonet. The hook caught in my enemy's jacket, and I could not get it out, although I stood on him. I had to loosen my bayonet stud, and I left the bayonet sticking in him. The British took the trenches, and the German dead outnumbered ours by about ten to one.

Neither side had completely broken the other in the opening battles of the war in Flanders and France. This stalemate saw both sides dig in and trench warfare ensued along what soon developed into a western front of 440 miles, extending from the Belgian coast to the Swiss border. The British were designated to hold 85 miles of front line between the Ypres Salient and the River Somme.

Pte Frederick William Heath had been a journalist on the *North Mail* in Newcastle until 1914 and became the first man from the office to see active service after he enlisted to 'do his bit' in 1/13th (County of London) Battalion, London Regiment. Writing to his editor from a field hospital 'somewhere in France' in November 1914, Heath paints an evocative picture of what day-to-day life was like in the trenches:

The weather is causing a good deal of trouble at present. We first get snow and frost, then a quick thaw, then another snap of frost, with bitter cold winds and perhaps rain. The effect of this on the trenches has been vile. When I was last in them four days ago, we were up to the calves in mud. Imagine me pushing my way through this with full pack and rifle until I get to my appointed post! Here I stick with my rifle, with bayonet fixed, through a loop hole cut out of earth heaped on top of the trench and stand on observation duty for two, four and six hours, as the case may be.

Generally it is two hours on and two hours off. When you are on, you have to keep your eye glued to the loophole and endeavour to spot any movement of men in the German trenches, the first of which is only 100 yards away from our trench. For the past week the enemy has been sapping right up to our trenches and it is believed that he is preparing some mine scheme to blow us out!

We see very little during the day, but at night those of us whose nerves are not good see a great deal. When I am off duty I crawl into a hole cut in the side of the trench and doubling myself up, pull a waterproof sheet – the soldier's best friend in the trenches – over me and try to snatch a little sleep. And so the night goes on. Comes the hour before daybreak, when we all stand to arms.

Cooking on a brazier, mealtime in the trenches, early 1916.

As soon as it is light, we get our fires going and begin to cook breakfast. Here is a typical day's menu:-

Breakfast – Bacon fried in our mess tin lids, bread roasted in the bacon fat, jam, butter, tea.

Dinner – Corned beef, cold or hot as you like; biscuits, bread and cheese, varied by camp ration containing tinned meat and vegetables.

Tea – Bread, butter and jam.

Of course many of us take up little luxuries of our own. But you will see how wonderfully fed we are. Then about 11 o'clock at night there is the rum parade. Neat rum it is and by jove! How we long for it! Of course, this will go on only so long as our transport can come up to the trenches. As things are at present, the transport halts in a ruined village only a couple of hundred yards behind our trenches. A ration party of about twenty men is detailed shortly after dusk and goes out to the transport and brings back the rations. It runs the risk of snipers, but one gets used to that.

The food is brought back in big wooden boxes and dumped down in the communication trench. In the morning, the rations for the day are given out. So our three days go on until on the evening of the third we pack up and stand by for orders to move out of the trenches. We are working at present in half battalions; one relieves the other. When the order comes to move we creep along the trench in single file and go out along the support trenches and into the road which leads to home or rather our billets six miles from the trenches.

When we begin to move out the other half moves in. It is all very well done but the danger lies in surprise attack. If the enemy attacked us as we were moving out there would be the very devil of a melee. Very soon we are out and on the slow march home for we are on the look-out for snipers and shells. This march back to billets always seems the longest thing in the world.

Some fall out but more of us stick for there is a fire in the linen factory where we stay, straw on the floor and blankets. The wet of the trenches is behind us except that brought away on our clothes (mine are caked with it now). Stew steams in the dixies [cooking pans]. Once in the billet off come the kits, out come the mess tins, down goes the stew! A pipe or cigarette, a little chatting over incidents and sleep – such as no man had before!

Christmas 1914 saw letters home and letters published in local newspapers telling of how the festive season was celebrated 'at the front'. One published in the *Morpeth Herald* had been sent home by 'a local nursing sister'; sadly her name was not published with it but it provides a rare insight into Christmas on an ambulance train:

Previous to receiving your letter and contents we had thought of trying to fill each patient on the train a 'Xmas Stocking' and make it to them as like Xmas at home as possible. But, thanks to you it was a much heavier stocking than it would have been, as we bought all sorts of nice things – big soft slippers for the poor frostbitten feet men, a big supply of oranges, toffee and chocolates; handkerchiefs and gloves for those going home on the boat etc., etc.

On Xmas Eve we went up to about 18 miles from the firing line, and I think it was the strangest Xmas one could possibly imagine. A glorious frosty night and such beautiful scenery one felt, in such a world, there could not possibly be a war going on. I put my head out of the carriage window about ten p.m. when we arrived at the rail-head where we were going to load. One heard the dull continuous thunder of the gun on one side and the sharp reports of rifles on the other: it seemed too awful for words on Christmas Eve. I just remarked to Sister it seemed as if the world had gone back to the uncivilised age again! One of our own Tommies on duty there, was delighted to see us and hailed me with: 'A Merry Christmas, Sister: glad to see you. Lovely night isn't it?' I felt ashamed of my sad thoughts and talked away to him and heard all the latest news until our patients began to arrive. They were delighted to get on the train, and oh, they did laugh when we gave them their Xmas stockings. We had previously filled about three hundred, a big family! One told me the last time he had hung his stocking up it was filled with cinders. We had an orange in each, cigarettes, handkerchief, toffee or chocolate, and a warm garment of some sort, and – I nearly forgot – some soap and notepaper. They were really like school-boys, and it did one good to see them with their coats absolutely laden with French earth – and such boots! They all got their Xmas stockings on and we got them nicely settled about 1 a.m. when the train started for the base.

Two of us went to bed then, and the other sister was on duty. I slept very soundly till 6, when I was wakened by hearing: 'Merry Christmas, Black Watch'. 'Same to you Worcester' – another train was passing ours, and they always have a shout at each other. Got up and had breakfast: my carriage mate fries the bacon on a paraffin stove we have and gets the table laid. (I may tell you it consists of three boards hammered together by a kindly "London Scottish" and covered with white linoleum). I am the washer-up. It is very convenient: she loves cooking and getting things ready, and I prefer the other so we fit in beautifully – in fact, the three of us are as happy a family as could be found the world over. We then did the dressings etc., until tea-time. The Major gave each of the men a Xmas card from the King and more cigarettes from himself, and I must not forget the Xmas pudding, with a bottle of stout each and fruit too. I think you will agree with me that Xmas Day was anything but dull here.

In the evening, when I went into the ward where we had our worst stretcher cases – thirty six of them all together – they were all singing in chorus and taking turns with the solos. Needless to say, I joined in too, and all agreed, in spite of 'Jack Johnsons' and Allemands, that Xmas was Xmas even in the ambulance train.

To-day (Sunday) we were down at one of the bases and were fortunate enough to get to church. It was a treat, and the wee English Church was decked with holly, and we had such a delightful sermon. Three parts of the congregation consisted of our own men, and, oh, it is grand to hear them all joining in 'God Save the King' – after the Benediction. It almost makes one weep. Everybody sings as if it were a prayer, not only a nation's prayer but his own – so hearty and stirring.

Princess Mary sent each of the Nursing Sisters on Xmas Day a charming box of chocolate. The box itself was guilt and on the lid her head in relief, with the names of the Allies in medallions surrounding it. Inside a very pretty card wishing us 'A Happy Christmas and a victorious New Year from Princess Mary and friends.'

The King and Queen's cards to all the troops, of which we each received one, are perfectly charming, with very good photographs of themselves and best wishes and signatures on the other side. Queen Alexandra sent each of us tea, biscuits and sweets.'

Above all, the festive season of 1914 will be remembered for the informal truce that occurred between British and German troops on Christmas Day. Corporal Robert Renton, Seaforth Highlanders, was there and wrote back to his parents, Mr and Mrs Renton of Fireburn Mill, Coldstream:

I never thought we could spend Christmas the way we did. We were in the trenches on Christmas Day. On Christmas Eve the Germans in front of us started singing what appeared to be hymns. We were shouting for encores – their trenches are only about 150 yards in front of us. They kept the singing up all night.

The ideal comforts to post to your special soldier at the front, 1914.

On Christmas Day some of them started to shout across to us to come over for a drink. It started with one or two going over halfway and meeting the Germans between the two lines of trenches. Then it got that there was a big crowd of Germans and British all standing together shaking hands and wishing each other a Merry Christmas.

They were giving us cigars and cheroots in exchange for cigarettes: and some of them had bottles of whisky. They seemed to be a decent crowd, those in front of us. They were all fairly well dressed, and the majority spoke broken English. Some of them could speak it as well as I can myself. They said that they were not going to fire for three days. They kept their word too. There was no rifle fire for two days after Christmas. There were two dead Frenchmen between our lines, and we could never get out to bury them until that day. The Germans helped us to dig the graves. One of their officers held a service over one of the graves. It was a sight worth seeing, and no one was forgotten.

The units involved in the truce were admonished for their behaviour by brigade and staff officers and sent away from those sectors of the line not to return 'for the duration' but truces and even live-and-let-live attitudes would regularly occur along the front during the rest of the war.

Driver Jack Murray of the Royal Field Artillery was so proud of his goatskin jerkin he sent a photo of himself wearing it while serving in France to his folks at Brighton Road, Gateshead.

Sgt John Bilcliffe of Violet Street, Benwell, had served with the Northumberland Fusiliers during the Anglo-Boer War (1899–1902) and rejoined 1st Battalion, Northumberland Fusiliers, just after the Battle of Mons. Bilcliffe was promoted from the rank of corporal after taking over command of a platoon who took a trench under formidable difficulties on 2 December 1914 and he felt great pride in the fact he was part of the first British unit to cross the Aisne, but the advance on Ypres, when fighting recommenced early in 1915, was to be his undoing:

The water was waist deep so we commandeered barrels from a neighbouring farm to stand – or rather crouch – on. Unnoticed, mine filled with water, and turned over open end up, into which I stepped, with what result may be imagined. Dead Germans so choked the trench, that only 17 could find room. For 48 hours, these held the enemy at 15 yards range, until relieved. My men left in perfect line, with the bullets pouring like rain.

A man benumbed and helpless with cold was carried by Tomsett and myself and being misled by a new construction of barbed wire along our lines, we lost our bearings and narrowly escaped falling into the enemy's hands. We ultimately reached our lines, but a long way from our regiment. The snipers are fearful, and very clever, managing to get all round us.

Bilcliffe discovered twenty-eight bullets through his coat, and three in his haversack, which he kept as souvenirs, but by some miracle he had not actually been wounded. Soon afterwards they were in action again and, with shells falling all around them, Bilcliffe was suddenly struck blind and would have walked straight into the German lines had he not been rescued by his comrade Sgt Lloyd. Bilcliffe was sent 'back to blighty' and spent two weeks in hospital at Brighton where they discovered he had also suffered the ill effects of frostbite to his feet. His eyesight began to return. The diagnosis was that he had temporarily lost his sight due to gun concussion.

Pte C. N. Loughman, 1st Battalion, Northumberland Fusiliers, was frank about life at the front and his experiences in the Ypres battle:

I have seen it said that the men are served with hot meals in the trenches but we did not get any where we were. We had to take it in turns to go out at night for food, and many men were killed on the journey. Then they say we play football! If a man has been right into the fighting line for a while, he does not feel like chasing a bit of leather about. He has had quite enough. It is really terrible work.

Sometimes the ammunition in the packs of the dead in front of the trenches is exploded by a stray shot, and the corpse's burn for hours at night, making a ghastly sight. Then it makes a man think when he sees his chums shot down by the side of him. On one occasion I was the only man left out of my platoon. One man I was with in India told me that he had come to the conclusion that it was no good dodging. If we had to be hit, we should be, and it was no use troubling. The next day he was struck and I had only time to clasp his hand before he passed away.

Such things as this sober one, but the British 'Tommy' cannot be quiet for long. He must joke about something to keep his mind off the darkest things, or there would soon be trouble. And so there is a good deal of 'leg pulling' in the trenches.

Blyth soldier Pte Leonard Short, of 2nd Battalion, Border Regiment, wrote home from the war hospital in the Central School, Aberdeen, where he was lying with a wound in the arm:

Just to let you know I arrived safe at Aberdeen from Southampton. The wound is getting on grand, but my arm is still useless on account of the broken bone. Another inch and I would have got it in the heart. We made a bayonet charge on the 23rd at La Bassee, and lost heavily again, but the Germans must have lost heavily too. I was wounded, and lay on the battlefield two hours before I got my arm bandaged, and I lost a lot of blood. My mate stuck to me all the time, but he dare not move for fear of getting shot himself, so we waited until the Borders returned victorious.

In a later letter from the hospital he recalled,

At Ypres we had some terrible fighting. We were alongside the Gordons, and had about ten hand-to-hand fights, and in one of them I got a punch on the nose from a German, but he got the bayonet for it. It was very dark at the time...'

I am getting on fairly well, and am out of bed, but I still feel weak. The people here are very kind, they come up to the hospital with fruit and everything. My arm is in splints now, and it pains a little, but I am putting up with it all with a good heart, because I have been very lucky in this way. I have done some hard fighting, and the Borders have made a name for themselves. At Ypres we fought 20 to I: charge after charge we made, driving the Germans back. Then the Kaiser brought the famous Guards and we fairly mowed them down like sheep. My hands and clothes were stained with blood for weeks without being washed. It was at this battle where our regiment was cut up. When the roll was called what a sight we looked, with only 300 men out of 1,200 men.

Pte John William Purvis, 2nd Battalion, Northumberland Fusiliers, returned to his home on Howard Street, North Shields, in April 1915 to recuperate after a stay in hospital. He was wounded at Ypres and gave an interview retold by the *Chronicle*:

Shrapnel from the enemy struck the soil two feet from him and he was carried a distance of four yard. When he came to he found himself buried in soil. There were four men lying dead near him and four yards away a comrade, also named Purvis (George), had both legs blown off. Pte Purvis was unable to render the poor fellow any assistance, being himself wounded and in a serious state from loss of blood.

There were six shrapnel bullets in the upper part of his left arm and five in the left shoulder. Purvis crawled back to the billet and rested till the next morning, when he told his officer that he thought he had been hit. The officer took him to a doctor, who removed his coat and found a great mass of blood in his clothing, upon seeing which the officer said: ' You told me you thought you had been hit. I think you have got a knock to last you for a bit'. ' I think he has,' said the doctor.

After spending one night in the temporary hospital Purvis was removed to the hospital at Le Touquet. This is entirely a Canadian institution, and of the Canadian doctors and nurses Purvis speaks in the highest terms. In two operations, six bullets were removed from his arm and shoulder.

After a month in the Canadian hospital, Purvis was shipped to England, and conveyed to Lincoln Hospital where he stayed one week, after which he came home. He has not yet recovered the use of his arm, and is receiving attention at the hospital in Percy Gardens, Tynemouth.

Pte John Purvis made a successful recovery from his injuries and returned to his old battalion, but sadly he was killed in action on 6 October 1918.

A newspaper cutting of a letter written by Pte William Gamblin of 9th Battalion, Durham Light Infantry, in the spring of 1915 was found pressed in the Book of Common Prayer he carried through the war:

We have just come out of the firing line for a well-earned rest and as soon as we got back we were visited by Sir John French and the General Staff and he gave us a fine address, thanking us for the fine work we had done. He said it was a pride to him to have in the Army under his command a Regiment which had shown such a daring front under heavy artillery fire. He said we had shown a fine example of bravery and coolness during the ten days we were under fire. He made most mention of one time we advanced across the open fields with the enemy's artillery peppering us and he congratulated us all, although I don't think for one moment our men understood what we had gone through until we came out of it. In fact we got so used to the shell fire that we did not take any notice of it. They would come whizzing over our heads and burst all about us. I think we could beat them back easily enough if they did not use the poison gases. There was one time they made an attack and all across the line we could see the poisonous gas coming on but they got the worst of it all the same.

Appeals from loving families for news of sons of all ranks missing in action frequently appeared in newspapers and the *St George's Gazette* throughout the war. Lt Alfred Piggott was eventually declared dead; he has no known grave and his name is carved on the Loos Memorial that commemorates 20,000 officers and men who have no know grave that fell in the area during the First World War.

20, BROADWATER DOWN,
TUNBRIDGE WELLS,

20th December, 1915.

DEAR SIR,—My son, Lieut. Arthur Alfred Piggot, 13th Service Batt. Northumberland Fusiliers, C. Coy., was reported wounded and missing by the War Office as between the 25th and 27th September last. So far as I have been able to ascertain Lieut. Piggot was wounded at about eleven o'clock on Sunday morning the 26th September, on Hill 70, Loos, France, and was left lying wounded on the Hill. I have heard a rumour that the Germans were seen carrying him away prisoner.

Any information will be gratefully received.

Yours faithfully,

J. ALFRED PIGGOT.

LIEUT. PIGGOT.

The Canny Lads of Choppington: A Soldier's Poem Sold on Postcards for a Penny Each

Composed at the front by Pte Albert Gibbons, No. 2050, 'D' Co., 4th Battalion, Northumberland Fusiliers (T.F):

Dear Tommy just a line or two,
To let you know that we've pulled through,
And to our country we'll be true,
The canny lads from Choppington.

To Blyth we came as strangers, but friends we parted,
And every lad was broken-hearted,
When on the boat for France we started,
The canny lads from Choppington.

We soon got face to face with Huns,
And their big Jack Johnson guns,
And they teemed the shrapnel in by tons,
On the canny lads from Choppington.

It just seemed to be our luck,
On we went with British pluck.
Till a piece of shrapnel came and struck
A canny lad from Choppington.

He faltered, then on his face he fell,
Beside him I knelt down as well,
And how he died just I can tell
That canny lad from Choppington.

Rather than being a German slave,
He lies on the field among the brave,
And I wrote on wood across his grave –
A canny lad from Choppington.

He volunteerd to cross the sea,
To fight for his king and country,
And fell for Englands Liberty –
That canny lad from Choppington.

Tell Thomas Davison, of Cowpen Quay,
And also Robert Caisley,

That you have had a line from me,
One of the lads from Choppington.

And tell them we are keeping fit,
As in our dug-outs here we sit,
Ready again to do our bit –
The canny lads from Choppington.

All the boys join in and send,
Their best respects to all their friends,
And on Providence it all depends –
For the canny lads from Choppington.

The men of the 16th (Service) Battalion, Northumberland Fusiliers, the 'Newcastle Commericals', had begun to wonder if they were going to 'miss the boat' for inclusion in action on the Western Front but get there they did, as their correspondent wrote to the *St. George's Gazette*, Regimental Journal of the Northumberland Fusiliers, in December 1915:

Out at last! The rugged towers of Alnwick Castle, the martial reviews of Cramlington, the dreamy sweetness of Catterick Bridge and the wearisome mountains of Codford seem to be dreams of the past; they fade into insignificance before the stearn reality of France. We were in the thick of it almost before we realised that our departure from England was on the tapis. The 16th were nevertheless not a whit the less keen than when they were in the prehistoric days of the 'Schools' and no amount of mud, water or rats will deter them from doing their utmost to live up to all the nice things that have been said about them.

Having censored some six-thousand letters, wiped a cup full of liquid mud from my face and hands and more or less successfully dodged about eighteen of the wily Hun's 'duds,' I take up my pen at the point where my predecessor left off. We spent many anxious hours before saying farewell to Codford and now a First Field Dressing and an identity disc proclaimed the rapid advent of the 'Day.' It came in the middle of the night, if one may be Hibernian, and we were whisked over the Channel packed like the proverbial sardines. Our history since we landed on French soil has been one long nightmare of route marches, billets and still more route marches. True, we occasionally shoot a German (or say we do) and work 'stunts' just to inform the enemy of our presence. But on the whole, life is pretty quiet and tolerable. It must be admitted that however depraved the modern Hun may be, he occasionally shows himself a sportsman by ceasing fire during breakfast time.

The town in which we rest is still a prey to German artillery, they won't leave us alone under any consideration. If we can't have a peaceful Christmas this year, we mean to make as much noise as possible.

If an outsider were to come across us today he would notice most of all the cheerful spirit of our men. To every hardship there is some comic relief and the man who sees the funny side of getting stuck up to the waist in slush or of dropping a Dixie of hot tea at the approach of a Bosche shell, hasn't much to fear.

Men of the 16th (Service) Battalion, Northumberland Fusiliers, in the wet trenches of the Western Front.

Between battles the front line would be quiet for long periods in the day. Soldiers in reserve or behind lines in a period of rest did take the time to write their own bawdy ballads and parody popular tunes, one of which caught on both in France and back in blighty, where it appeared in numerous magazines, newspapers and even on postcards. It was written by Pte Michael Riley of 1st Battalion, Northumberland Fusiliers, formerly of Heaton, who sent his original parody of 'My Little Grey Home in the West' in a letter to his uncle in Gateshead in 1915.

My Little Wet Home in a Trench

I've a little home in a trench,
Where the rainstorms continually drench;
There's the sky overhead,
Clay or mud for a bed,
And a stone that we use for a bench.

Bully Beef and hard biscuits we chew,
It seems years since we tasted a stew;
Shells cackle and scare,
Yet no place can compare,
With my little wet home in the Trench.
Our friends in that trench o'er the way,
Seem to know that we've come here to stay,

They shoot and they shout
But they can't get us out
Though there's no dirty trick they won't play.
They rushed us a few nights ago
But we don't like intruders, and so,
Some departed quite sore,
Others left ever more,
Near my little wet home in the Trench.

So hurrah for the mud and the clay,
Which leads to Der Tag, that's The Day
When we enter Berlin,
That City of Sin,
And make the fat Berliner pay

Yes, we'll think of the cold, slush and stench,
As we lay with the Belgian and French
There'll be shed then, I fear,
Redder stuff than a tear,
For my Little Wet Home in the Trench.

One of thousands of military greetings cards printed by R. Johnson & Son of Gateshead that were sent to and from the soldiers at the front during the First World War.

In tough times and adverse conditions it was not the time for a sense of humour failure, as Capt. C. H. Cooke M. C. wrote in his *Historical Records of the 16th (Service) Battalion, Northumberland Fusiliers:*

On 26 January 1916 the whole battalion moved back to Millencourt where a new front line was required in front of the old one. To enable this to be carried out quickly two large parties were required, one for digging, the other for wiring. 'Expert wirers and hefty diggers were selected from each of the battalions in the Brigade and after some practice proceeded on the evening of 2 February to carry out this scheme. Captain Dunglinson and Lieutenant Wake were in charge of the wiring party. The work was done exceedingly well, the wire was completed and the trench dug six feet deep on the first night. The most uncomfortable conditions could not repress the Tynesider's humour. It was a blessing that they could see the funny side of affairs that would have otherwise caused a mental collapse. One wiring party had been out some time in 'No Man's Land' and had succeeded in erecting a creditable obstacle of barbed wire. On receiving the order to return to the trench, one party looked proudly at the finished job and remarked to his officer: 'It'll be a bloody cliver cat that gets into wor garden eftor this war, sor'.

One of the few trench numbers of *The Growler*, the humorous magazine of the 16th (Service) Battalion, Northumberland Fusiliers, published while they were in the trenches on the Western Front.

It certainly seems like there were some likely lads in the battalion's wiring parties. On another occasion instructions had been received to erect a barbed wire entanglement over a small mound in front of the line.

Work was duly begun one cold and frosty night and as the enemy was not far away every precaution was taken to ensure quick and silent work. Presently the O.C. discovered that there were no more iron screw pickets and whispered to a hardy Northumbrian miner to crawl back and get some. This man had almost reached the top of the mound on his return journey when his foot slipped on the frozen surface and down he rolled with his burden of iron stakes and barbed wire coils. Immediately fire was opened by the enemy in the direction of all the noise and the wiring party lay as close to mother earth as they could get. But the cause of all the commotion having rolled to the foot of the hill sat bolt upright and in a loud Northumbrian voice demanded 'Did ye see that slip, sor? Aa might ha' been killed.'

St Eloi

The attack to consolidate the newly blown mine craters at St Eloi, south-east of Ypres, on 27 March 1916 by 1st Battalion, Northumberland Fusiliers, is etched bold in the history of our county regiment, not because it was an outstanding victory or significant achievement, although achievements were indeed made – the Northumberland Fusiliers, deployed on the right flank of the attack, reached the German wire with the loss of only one soldier. Other battalions in the attack were less fortunate and it

One of a series of photographs that became nationally famous during the First World War showing the men of 1st Battalion, Northumberland Fusiliers, after the attack on St Eloi, 27 March 1916.

became a hard-fought battle to consolidate the final crater, which was finally captured by 8th Battalion, The King's Own, in the early hours of 3 April.

St Eloi stands out for the Northumberland Fusiliers simply because it was so well documented by wartime press photographers. Even a film, believed to be the first to be shot of a British attack, was taken by Lt Geoffrey Malins, one of the War Office's kinematographers. In the footage Northumberland Fusiliers, some wearing their war trophies, can be clearly seen escorting hundreds of prisoners taken after the battle. In the final sequence the Northumberland Fusiliers are back in their rest area and official war photographer Ernest Brooks is seen moving through them; once off camera he encourages them to cheer for the photograph. The lasting legacy of the images he took is that even a century on they remain some of the most iconic photographs of front line soldiers after action during the First World War.

April 1916 saw the Service Battalions of the Northumberland Fusiliers celebrate their first St George's Day in the trenches. Typical of them were the 19th (Service) Battalion, Northumberland Fusiliers (Pioneers), who wrote to the editor of the *St George's Gazette*:

Since the last notes were written we have moved twice and are back where we were. It is a cheerful pastime this moving and no-one seems to gain anything tangible … In the interval between the losing and regaining of this paradise the Battalion organised and conducted a Divisional School of Field Engineering where tired infantry officers and N.C.Os back for 'rest' were instructed in the art of coaxing sandbags and avoiding barbed wire. Night work making entanglements proved a very useful exercise. The tailors were kept busy afterwards. Casualties have been few and the health of the men is excellent. Preparations are now being made to celebrate St. George's Day and the Battalion should present a gay appearance when decked out with the roses kindly sent by the Chamber of Commerce Committee.

Soldiers of the Northumberland Fusiliers proudly wearing their red and white roses to mark St George's Day during the First World War.

The Committee have also sent tobacco and sweets; while the Elswick and Scotswood workmen have generously provided cake, sweets, etc. These gifts are great appreciated by all.

Spirits are high. By some chance one of the men 'discovered' that the 115th Wurtemburgers were in front. Correct or not, he was anxious to impart the news and in delightful Northumbrian, he called to his mate:

'De ye knaa whe's in front?'

'No.'

'Why, just the 115 wooden buggers!'

The battalions were soon back in action and suffering more tragic losses. This deeply moving poem is dedicated 'In Memory of My Brother Pte, Ernest Plumb, who was Killed by my Side on 25 May 1916.'

Standing in a traverse
Were two brothers true;
Whilst over our parapet
The German trench mortar flew.

They were two young "Terriers,"
Who volunteered to go
Out to the battlefields of Flanders.
To face the foreign foe.

Only a scream of warning,
Only a bursting mortar shell,
Which parting these two brothers.
Till when, no one can tell.

They went to war unheeding.
With many a parting cheer;
Left at home their loved ones,
And each a vacant chair.

In a soldiers' graveyard,
A wooden cross was put next day,
And on it – "Killed in Action
On the Twenty-fifth of May"

You can guess what it meant to me,
To see my brother's soul lie there;
But our Lord Almighty had called him.
And he answered without a fear.

When the war is over,
Remembered he will be,

By mother, father, brothers and sisters
And ever so by me.

So don't get down-hearted all,
For he gave his life to help to save
His King and Country so dear,
And won honour in a soldier's grave.

Written by his brother, L/Cpl Charles Plumb.

The Plumb brothers were the sons of John and Sarah Plumb of Wallsend. Pte Ernest Plumb of 1st/5th Battalion, Northumberland Fusiliers, was buried in La Laiterie Military Cemetery, Belgium. His brother, Charles, who wrote the poem, was killed five months later on the 27 October 1916. He was twenty-three years old. The poem and story were printed and sold to raise money for war charities.

Orders and Kit for the First Day of the Somme, 1 July 1916

Excerpts from the operational order by Lt-Col. Lyle, commanding the 23rd Battalion, Northumberland Fusiliers (4th Battalion, Tyneside Scottish), dated 21 June 1916:

ADVANCE – Once the attack is launched it must be pressed forward at all costs until the final objective of the battalion is reached.

The extreme importance of a resolute advance must be clearly impressed on all ranks and the advance must continue regardless of whether other units on our flanks are held up or delayed.

The aim of each wave must be to support and where necessary carry forward the wave in front, until the ultimate objective allotted to the Battalion is reached…

The frontage to be covered by each line in the advance is approximately 450 yards, therefore as soon as the attack is launched each line will extend to 2 paces interval.

DRESS & EQUIPMENT

Every man will carry:
Rifle and equipment (less pack)
2 extra bandoliers of S.A.A.
2 Mill's Grenades (1 in each side pocket)
1 iron ration and rations for the day of assault
Haversack and waterproof cape
Four sandbags
2 gas helmets and 1 pair Spicer Goggles
Either a pick or a shovel (excepting bombers and signallers)

Full water-bottle

Mess tins to be carried in haversack.

Bomb buckets, bomb waistcoat carrier and wire cutters will be distributed under the supervision of O.C. Companies.

Bombers to carry equipment ammunition only.

DISTINGUISING MARK

All ranks will wear an equilateral triangle of yellow cloth 16 inch sides attached to the back, base upwards.

IRON RATIONS

All ranks are reminded that iron rations are not to be eaten without definite orders from an officer. If it is necessary to use Iron Rations only one ration for every three men is to be opened. If more are found to be required a second tin can then be opened. The number of Iron Rations used to be reported every six hours

WATER It is extremely difficult to carry up water and all ranks must be clearly warned that drink water is economised as much as possible. All Officers are responsible that this is done.

STRETCHER BEARERS & WOUNDED Before the assault is delivered the Battalion Aid Post will be established in the Front Line near KEATS REDAN. All stretcher bearers will report to the Medical Officer on night Y/Z time to be notified later. During the advance stretcher bearers will remain under the M.O. All ranks must be clearly warned that men are on no account to assist the wounded.

PRISONERS Prisoners of War will be passed back as the situation allows to Brigade Collecting Station established at the Headquarters of the Right Battalion (Chape Spur) where they will be handed over to the guard.

MISCELLANEOUS (I) No papers or orders are to be carried by Officers or men taking part in the attack except the new 1/5000 German Trench Map and the 1/20,000 Map Sheet 57d.S.R. All messages and reports will refer to one or the other of these maps.

(II) Hand Grenades are difficult to replenish, they must not be thrown indiscriminately.

(III) Captured Machine Guns must be collected or damaged.

(IV) Pipers will accompany their companies.

(V) All maps etc. referred to in these orders are to be seen at Battalion Headquarters.

After months of the routine of the trenches, suffering bitter cold, wet, mud, bodily infestations such as lice, losing mates to trench fever, trench foot, sickness, drop shorts, snipers, raiding parties or just plain bad luck, the men on the Western Front were clamouring for a big push, something that would strike a blow that would mean the beginning of the end of the war, but they were under no illusion that it would cost many of them their lives.

Pte John Scollen, 27th (4th Tyneside Irish) Battalion, Northumberland Fusiliers, wrote home on the eve of the Battle of the Somme (there are gaps in the letter because it was treasured over many years, folded and creased, worn through in places and held together with yellowed sticky tape):

My Dear Wife and Children it is with regret I write ... last words of farewell to you we are about ... a charge against these ... Germans if it is God's Holy will that I should fall ... Have done my duty to my King and Country and ... Hope justly in the sight of God it is hard to part from you but keep a good heart dear Tina and do not grieve for me for God and his Blessed Mother will watch over you and my bonny little children and I have not the least doubt but that my Country will help you ... for the sake of one of its soldiers that ... his duty.

Well Dear Wife Tina I would ask ... I have never had cause because you have ... good wife and mother to look after my canny bairns and I'm sure they will be a credit to both of us.

Dearest wife Christina accept this little souvenir of France a cross made from a French bullet which I enclose for you.

My Joe, Jack, Tina and Aggie not forgetting my bonny little twins Nora and Hugh and my last flower baby whom I have only had the great pleasure of seeing ... since he came into the world God bless them ... I will try to get to my duty ... on this perilous undertaking and if I ... a xx on top of this missive so that you will know that I died in Gods holy Grace tell all my friends and yours also that I bid ... farewell now my dear wife and children I have not anything more to say only I wish you all Gods Holy Grace and Blessing so GOOD BYE GOOD ... and think of me in your prayers I know ... hard words for to receive but Gods will be done.

From your faithful soldier, husband and father, John Scollen B Coy S.B.N.F.
Good Bye my loved ones. Don't cry.

Pte John Scollen was posted missing presumed dead after 1 July 1916. He is named on the Thiepval Memorial to the Missing.

Pte Ernest Watson of 16th (Service) Battalion, Northumberland Fusiliers, 'the Newcastle Commercials', wrote back about his experiences on the first day on the Somme:

At last I have an opportunity to write you a short account of my experiences since 'the day' – July 1st. As you no doubt know, our battalion was the first to go over the top in our Brigade. However, to begin at the beginning, on Friday night, June 30th: we left our bivouacs and marched to the trenches, arriving in the front line about 11 p.m. It had been arranged that we were to go over at 2 a.m. on the following morning, but shortly after arrival word came along that this arrangement was cancelled and we were not going over till 7.30 a.m. Our artillery had been bombarding continuously for a week and now this was increased and the din was terrific. Jimmy (my brother-in-law who joined with me at the Grammar School) and I found a deep dug-out and lay down to make the most of the time we had before going over. Next morning I was awakened at 7.00 and told the battalion was about to go over, so I collected my things (rifle, bayonet, equipment, 240 rounds of ammunition, 2 bombs, 2 gas helmets, and shovel) and went out. It was a lovely morning with the sun shining gloriously. The noise was deafening, and the air was absolutely full of flying missiles. One had to shout to be heard. I cannot say I felt at home, but must confess it was one of the most awful experiences I have had. At 7.30 word came along for No. 1 platoon to go over. It was a grand sight to see them go over, but at the same time sad. Not one of them hesitated. At intervals of a few minutes 2 and 3 platoons followed, and then word came along for No 4 platoon to go over. I had just turned to get hold of my rifle which was standing against the parados when something burst just above me and a piece of shrapnel hit me in the mouth, and dust and earth nearly blinding me for the time being. I later found the roof of my mouth was also slightly damaged. Jimmy dragged me to a dug-out close at hand and then he went over the top. There were already two other wounded in this dug-out, one hit in the arm and the other in the leg – both shrapnel wounds. One of our runners brought in word that the boys had not been able to get much further than our own barbed wire. The Germans had been quite prepared and expecting us, for no sooner had our first wave appeared over the parapet than they mounted their own parapet and absolutely mowed our men down … To give you an idea of what the 16th were up against, I may say their objective has not been taken yet. I heard afterwards that after lying out between the lines all day, what remained of the battalion was withdrawn after dark to our own trenches.

Pte George Charlton wrote back about his experience going over the top with the Tyneside Scottish on the first day on the Somme:

I am all right after our gallant charge, and thank God for bringing me safely back. We got a severe dressing. We have been addressed by our Brigadier-General, who says he is proud of us, and the Tyneside Scots will never die. We have also been addressed by the Army Corps Commander, who spoke more flatteringly than our Brigadier. We held the trenches during the eight days bombardment previous to going over the top, which was enough to break any man down. As far as I am able I will give my experiences.

I was up all the Friday night helping in the issue of stuff, and about 4 a.m. had to go with hot tea and bacon for the men's breakfasts. At 7 o'clock we were told to prepare for a big mine going off, and at 7.20 up it went. What a sight! Earth and smoke were flying heavenwards, and we were nearly shaken to pieces. The waiting to get away was awful.

When orders came to advance, what a change there was! Every man rushed to the ladders to get over. You shook hands with a pal, wished him the best of luck, and over the top. The German artillery was awful, but – some smoking tabs, others cheering, and all smiling – over we went, the pipers playing 'The Campbells are Coming'. Some poor souls were killed before we got away, but we took no notice, as we must get on. On all sides men were falling, but on we went over our lines into 'No Man's Land', which was the ground between the opposing lines. It was simply awful, but you had to take no notice. We were also catching the Germans machine-gun fire, which made things worse, and the ground was simply ploughed up with shell.

What a good job our artillery had blown their wire to pieces, so that we could get over canny and mount the first line German trench. How anyone lived to get over I don't know. The first thing I saw was our bombers at work in the German dug-outs. After getting our wind we prepared to take the second line. I don't know what I felt like. I think no one was in his right senses; the sights were enough to turn anyone's brain. All I seem to remember was jumping over the parapet, and yelling at the top of my voice.

No sooner did we show ourselves than the machine guns were opened on us. Men fell on all sides, but we managed to get the second line.

Captain John 'Jack' Macfarlane Charlton, 21st (Service) Battalion, Northumberland Fusiliers (2nd Battalion Tyneside Scottish). A man of high artistic and literary talents, and a keen naturalist, he had published a number of works on ornithology, including *The Birds of South East Northumberland*, before the war. Jack was killed in action on the first day of the Somme. His elder brother, Hugh, had been killed just days earlier on 24 June.

Then came the order to take the third line, and over the top we went again, but the machine gun fire was awful. When about five yards from the trenches I staggered and fell into a shell hole, where two of our men were. They asked where I was hit, but I was only dazed, and they left me. At night I found out the reason why I fell. A piece of shrapnel went right through my haversack, then through a leather purse, through my ration bag among my biscuits, through the side of a tin of Oxo cubes, and out of the lid, but never hurt me. I lay there, and dare not move. If I showed my head a bullet came whistling back. I stayed there until it became unbearable, so I decided to crawl back to the second line.

With a prayer on my lips, away I crept, and luckily I managed to get in and joined our chaps. We now mounted the fire step in the second line, and made our position secure. As I was on the fire step some of the German bombers came down the third line after our lads. Three of them were together, and when they showed themselves, I took aim and fired just as one of them was about to fire at our men, and sent him to meet his Maker.

We had an anxious time then, as the Germans might counter-attack before we got reinforcements. Our water was finished, and we got orders to eat our emergency rations. But relief arrived, and the order came 'Tyneside Scots clear out, and let your relief get their reinforcements up'. We saw them go over the top into the German third line, and then we got out to make room for the next line of men. We had to get back over 'No Man's land', where we were shelled again, but I manged to get back, and went straight to our cook, who had a nice drink of tea ready for us. We then marched to headquarters, where they gave us supper, and afterwards we went into a big barn to sleep.

The artillery officers who saw us go over declared it to be the finest charge ever seen. Even the German prisoners who were brought in, said they had never seen anything like it in the war. I am pleased we have done our duty nobly and well, and offer my sympathies to all who have fallen so bravely. Now it is over, it just seems like a horrible dream. Let us hope the end is in sight, and that we will soon be back to our beloved ones at home.

Pte Robert Walker of the Tyneside Scottish, who was wounded in action on the first day of the Somme, wrote home to his wife at No. 12 Coronation Street, North Shields, from his bed in Chester Hospital:

We had been in the trenches for 14 days, and we should have made our attack on the 29th June, but it was put off till the morning of July 1st. Well, we took up our position at 2 o'clock in the morning. We were up to the knees in mud and water. We got a tot of rum and a drop of cold tea, but it was awfully cold tea, and we had not to make the attack till 7.30. At 6 o'clock we started to shell the German first line trench. This put the Germans on their guard, because they knew we were coming. It fell to the luck of the Tyneside Scottish to lead the charge of the Division. The Tyneside Irish had to follow us. Now 7.30 came, and over we went with the pipers playing. We had about 600 yards to go for the first line of the German trenches, but as soon as we showed our heads the German machine guns started, and hundreds of our men were shot down before we got away from our own trenches. The shots were striking the ground the same as you see a heavy fall of hailstones. It was then I hardly knew how I was doing it, but I kept my eyes off those that were falling in case I saw anybody I knew, for if I had it might have affected my spirits, so on I went, and before very long I was engaged with the Germans in their first line. We got this cleared out of them, and went on to his second line. It was here that I got shot through the hip, and I thought it was time to clear out, so I looked about me, and found only about 50 of us, and the ground covered with dead and wounded. The rest of the troops must have got orders to retire, so I started to limp away, and I got over his first line again, but in doing so I got another shot, under my right arm. They were both lucky shots. After I got out of his trenches, I found that he was shooting our wounded that were lying about, and I could walk no farther, so I got in a shell hole, threw all my gear off, took out my bandages and tied up my hip, but I could not tie up my arm. After this was done I peeped out of the hole to see if there was any chance of getting away. To do so would have meant death, so I had to content myself where I was. I lay there all day Saturday in the burning sun, and dare not move in case a German sniper might see me. I lay there all day without a drink of water or bite to eat, and with the loss of blood I was very weak. I lay from 8 o'clock in the morning till dark. Then I made a bid for my life, I had about 500 yards to crawl on my hands and knees, and the worst of it was I did not know which direction to make for, but I started off, and was gasping for water, and the only way I got it was to crawl up to dead men and get a drink form their water bottles; but at last I got into our lines at break of day on Sunday morning. Then I found our trench dug outs were all full of wounded, and I did not get out till Monday morning. All the time I had nothing to eat, but a good heart goes a long way. I could have had a nice helmet for Bobbie, but I know he would rather have his dad. Now I am quite comfortable and doing well.

Cpl Bob Kennedy, 27th (Service) Battalion, Northumberland Fusiliers, 4th Tyneside Irish, also wrote to his wife Florence describing events on the Somme – his right elbow had been shattered so the letter was written with his left hand:

We arrived in the assembly trench shortly after midnight where we waited until the time of attack. Our artillery kept up a heavy fire all night, until just turned 6 o'clock when every gun we had opened fire, it was hell let loose, they kept it up until 7.27 a.m. when we fired the first mine, 3 minutes after we fired our large mine, my God I should not have liked to be there it made the earth tremble. That was the signal we were waiting. 'Over the top and best of luck' was the cry. So over we went only to meet a perfect storm of machine gun fire. Then our lads began to fall, the first to fall was a chum by my left side called Nicholson of Ellison St. Gateshead, then my bosom pal Sgt Hall.

Soldiers of the Tyneside Irish Brigade advancing towards the enemy lines, first day of the Somme, 1 July 1916.

Pals from 16th (Service) Battalion, Northumberland Fusiliers 'Newcastle Commercials', shortly before the first day on the Somme, 1916.

After that my memory was not very clear, I was seeing blood until I was in the thick of it in the German lines. It did not take us long to get the best of it there. On looking my men up I found that there were only 3 of us left of my platoon, however as I was the senior N.C.O. left, I took charge of all the men around about which there were a mixed lot of all regiments. We advanced and took the German third line with very little trouble, but Fritz started then to bomb without doing much damage, it was here they nearly got me with a bomb. I was inspecting the line when we almost ran into a strong German bombing party but as luck would have it we saw them first and made them a present of nearly a dozen which gave them quite a turn, however one of theirs almost got me, seeing it coming I just had time to step back into the next bay when it went off. On returning down the line I met my Captain to whom I reported the work done and the work in hand. However as many more stragglers had come in, the Captain decided to attack the fourth line, so over the top we went again to be met by heavy machine gun fire, which took a heavy toll, my Captain among the many. It proved too hot, we were driven back to the third line. My Captain was lying out there between us and the Germans, so two of us went out and carried him to a shell hole where I dressed him, then we crawled back to our chums. After seeing the Captain safe I went along the trenches and it was on returning that a sniper got me. I reported to the Captain then made my way back to the German front line to try to get back to our own line. However, that was impossible for he was shelling No Man's Land, so an officer of the R.A.R. advised me to go into a dugout until night. The first two I passed were full of wounded, the next which had been for officers was empty, so the other two chums and myself went down stairs, it was about 30ft down below the ground. What was our surprise to hear a voice cry 'Mercy Camerade' and a big German got off one of the beds, he was slightly wounded in the forearm and leg, there was another one on a bed but he was dying, there were 6 beds in the first room and as far as I could see 4 in the second. The prisoner was very kind to me, he brought me soda water and chocolate. I lay until 4 o'clock and as I was losing blood I decided to run the risk and so I and my chums went over the top and made our way back arriving at the first station at 6.00 p.m. From there I walked another mile where I got the motor. It was here I got a drink of tea, the first since the night before. I arrived at the operation place at 8.00 p.m. where I lay outside until 11.00 p.m. After coming from the table I lay until 3.00 a.m. Sunday waiting to be taken to hospital. Arrived Heilly 5 o'clock, left for Romel at 11.00 a.m., left 2.00 p.m. next day 3rd July for England by HM Hospital Ship *St. George*, arrived here 8.00 p.m. 4th July. So that is the best rough outline I can give you dear.

With love, Bob '

The officer helped by Cpl Kennedy was Capt. Ralph Broomfield Pritchard who wrote to thank him from his bed in Ward B7 at the Military Hospital, High Street, Manchester:

My dear Kennedy

I am delighted to hear you have landed safe and sound in 'Blightie.' How's the arm? I hope the wound is not serious and you will soon be better. My wound turned out to be a flesh wound right through my rear and beyond a good deal of discomfort I am going on nicely and hope to be better in a fortnight. I stayed in the line until about 6.00 p.m. and with Bond's assistance made my way out to the right but I did not get a stretcher until I was opposite the middle of Beevant Wood.

I believe there are under 50 of our Battalion left and no Officers who went over except the Colonel but I do not think any officers have been killed. I have often wondered if you managed to get out all right and have very grateful memories of all you did for me.

The 27th (4th Tyneside Scottish) Battalion, Northumberland Fusiliers, suffered the third worst casualties of any battalion on the first day of the Somme (only the 1st Newfoundlands and 10th West Yorkshire Regiment suffered more). In the 4th Tyneside Scottish alone there were nineteen officers and 610 men killed and wounded on the first day of the Somme.

Capt. Ralph Pritchard recovered from his injury, returned to his battalion in September 1916 and was made adjutant – he was mentioned in despatches. Robert Kennedy was given an honourable discharge in February 1917 for the wound he received. Capt. Pritchard went on to be decorated with the Military Cross and the Distinguished Service Order but he was killed in action on 26 April 1918.

Mrs Connolly of No. 225 Commercial Road, Byker, received the following letter from her husband, CQMS John Connolly, who was in Wharncliffe Hospital,

Sheffield, after he was wounded while heading into action with 24th (Service) Battalion, Northumberland Fusiliers (1st Battalion, Tyneside Irish), when he was wounded on 1 July 1916:

I would like to say a word or two about the regiment. We went over the top of our trenches, and made the German trenches in good order. It was splendid, and good courage was displayed. Many of the officers and senior N.C.O.'s were down early on. It was marvellous. I saw a young lance-corporal taking a section up as coolly as if they were on parade. He was knocked down in front of me. I got hit myself, just a minute afterwards, but I could still see them moving up and falling fast, worse luck. You know how the old Fifth kept up its traditions. Well, the Tyneside Irish lived up to them on Saturday morning, July 1. The pity of it is that so many of them were mowed down in upholding the name of the 'Old and the Bold'. They were a credit to the old country. The nearest and dearest of those that are no more, when their first sorrow is over, can say with pride, 'He was one of the Tyneside Irish.

Recommended for the Victoria Cross–a Lost Hero of the First Day on the Somme

John Weldon had been working as a joiner in Newcastle when he joined the 'Newcastle Commericals' in September 1914. He always stood out as a good soldier and by 1 July 1916 he was Company Sergeant Major of No. 6 Platoon, B Company, 16th Battalion, Northumberland Fusiliers. He went over the top with his company at Thiepval at 7.30 a.m. and when all his officers were either killed or wounded, he took charge and did not return to his own trenches until 10.45 p.m. During the day he continually sniped away at the enemy and was officially known to have killed or wounded twenty-nine Germans. Despite his rifle being shot out of his hands on two occasions, he picked up the abandoned rifles of his fallen comrades and carried on. During the afternoon, while still under heavy fire, he crawled from shell hole to shell hole dressing the wounds of injured soldiers from his company and got no less than fifteen badly wounded lads back to British lines. His commanding officer, Lt-Colonel William H. Ritson, went on record to say 'Weldon's conduct throughout this terrible day was magnificent ... His action was worthy of a Victoria Cross but that recommendation as in many other cases has not been granted.' His gallantry was, however, recognised with the award of a Distinguished Conduct Medal.

Sadly Weldon later ended up in a hospital that was bombed and sustained further injuries during the raid from which he died on 3 September 1917, He lies in Wimereux Communal Cemetery, France. He was thirty-two years old. Not having lived to receive his DCM, it was presented to his family at a special event at Newcastle Exchange where Col. Ritson pinned the medal onto the coat of Weldon's little daughter and fine tributes were paid to this brave soldier.

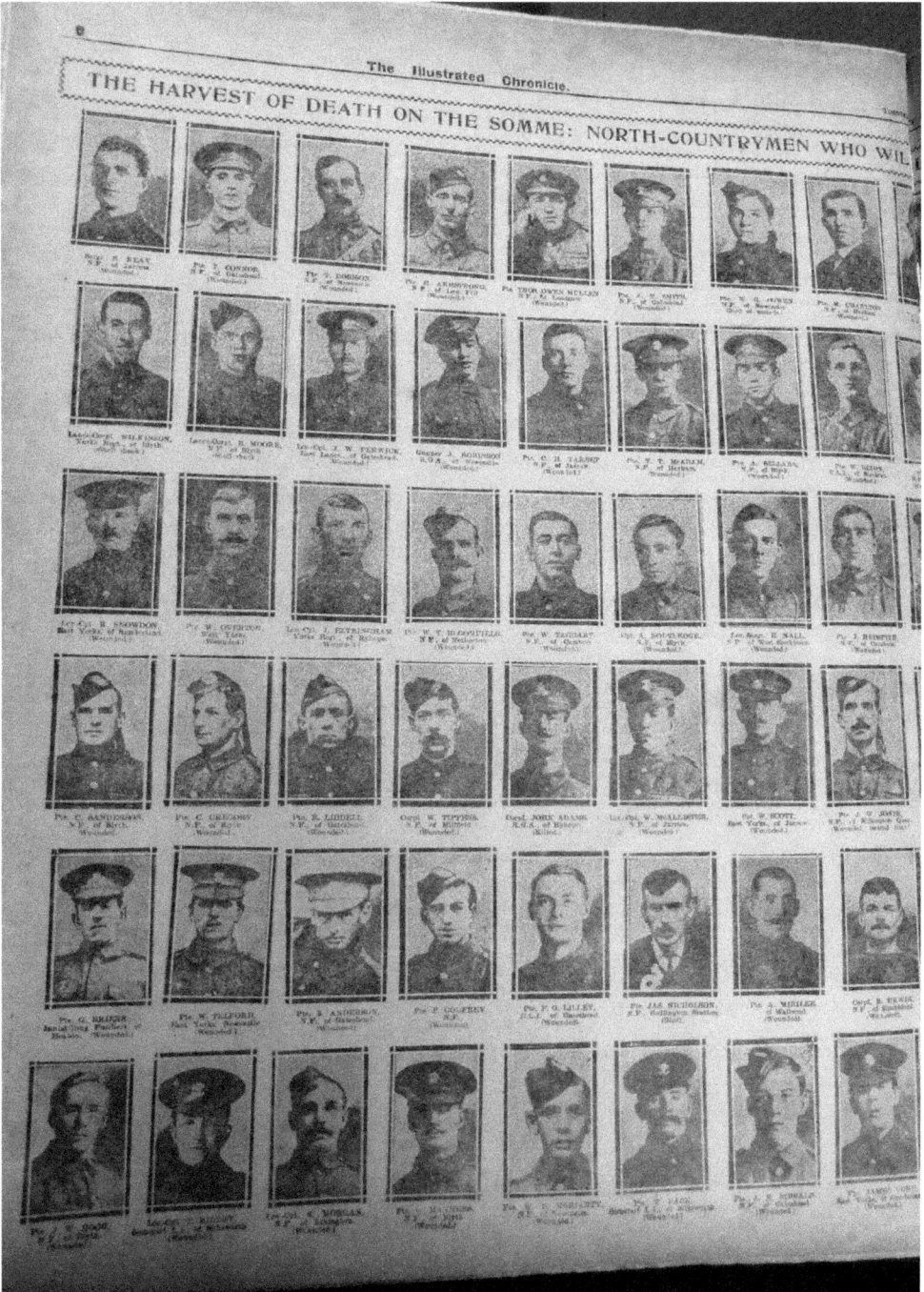

One of numerous pages showing the portraits of the killed and wounded of the first day of the Somme published in the Newcastle *Illustrated Chronicle* for many days after the carnage suffered by our local battalions on 1 July 1916.

I Regret to Inform You...

After the first day of the Somme thousands of letters were sent to the next of kin of the sons of Northumberland who had died. Everyone knew someone who had been injured or had been killed, and in some instances whole communities went into mourning. Here are just three of those stories.

A brother officer wrote to the parents of Lt John Hylton Patterson of 23rd (4th Tyneside Scottish) after 1 July 1916:

Dear Mr Patterson,

It is with the greatest regret that I write to inform you that your son was killed during the attack in La Boiselle, on July 1st. The Tyneside Scottish Brigade were ordered to attack the German lines on both sides of the village, and they went forward with great dash and spirit, but were met with a terrific storm of machine gun bullets, and shrapnel, and a very large percentage of officers and men fell. The German trenches were eventually entered, and our brigade reached the third line, but they were obliged to fall back to the first line until reinforcements came up, when the third line was again taken and consolidated.

I was talking to John a few minutes before he went over to attack, and he was quite cheerful and confident. I did not see him again, but afterwards saw his orderly, who was with him to the end, and who told me that he was wounded first of all, but he bravely struggled to a sitting position and urged his men on. Whilst he was shouting words of encouragement he was fatally struck by a bullet. In the meantime his orderly was badly wounded, being hit in three places.

Out of all the officers of our battalion who went into the attack, I am sorry to say that only two got back all right – myself and another lieutenant.

John was a very great personal friend of mine, and in the same company, and I feel very deeply for you in your bereavement. It will give you great pleasure and pride to know that he was loved and respected by his men, who followed and fell with him in the field. Again accept my deepest sympathies in your time of trouble – Yours sincerely, G.S. Nelson, Lieut.

Mr Farquhar Laing, father of twenty-six-year-old Capt. Dudley Ogilvie Laing of the 22nd (3rd Tyneside Scottish) Battalion, Northumberland Fusiliers, had some hope. His son was reported missing after the first day of the Somme; a week later the telegram arrived officially reporting him killed in action. A letter also arrived from his son's Company Sergeant Major, dictated from his hospital bed, explaining the circumstances of Capt. Laing's death:

When the order was given to advance Captain Laing and myself were over at once, the men following smartly. Five minutes after the Captain was wounded on the neck and fell and had to be left. He came round, however and came on again and was again bowled over and was not seen to move any more. Later on his orderly went out to try and get him brought in but reported him as dead and he could not get the body moved. I am sorry not to give Mr Laing further information. I myself was badly wounded and could do nothing to help. Tell him please that the Captain was one of the best, liked by his brother officers and held the respect and esteem of the men and to me it is as though I had lost a friend, let alone my Captain.

Pte Alexander Currie (formerly of a miner Horden and a native of South Shields) had already gone out under heavy fire and had successfully brought in fourteen wounded soldiers during the action, and when Capt. Laing's body had been located he again went out alone in an effort to reach him, but the fire grew too intense and he had to give up the attempt. Currie was later decorated with the Military Medal for Bravery in the Field for his actions on that day. Sadly the body of Capt. Dudley Laing, like so many of our men, was never recovered and his name joins those of over 70,000 other lads from the British regiments that fought on the Somme on the Thiepval Memorial to the Missing.

This last, poignant story was told in the *Illustrated Chronicle* of a popular local lad, a real 'boy next door' who was doing well in life and on the football field:

Mr. J. H. Dunglinson of Balmoral, Moorside, Fenham, was notified Saturday that his youngest son, Corporal Dan Dunglinson of the Northumberland Fusiliers is missing. He is one of three sons who joined on 6 September 1914 and went to France on 22 November 1915. He took part in the great British advance on 1 July. He was one of the first to jump when the order to charge was given and was one of the first to fall, since when he has not been heard of. Corporal Dunglinson was a well-known local footballer, commencing his career with the Brighton West End and assisting that club to win the Northern Amateur League, 1909–10. Before the war he played as amateur full back for Newcastle United. He was reserve man for an amateur team which played the Germans at Berlin and was also with the local team at The Hague. In January 1914 he was in civil life employed at the Goods Audit Office of the N.E.R. Company at Newcastle. Another son of Mr. Dunglinson's is Captain Victor Dunglinson who was wounded last month and is now going on well. A third son (William) is still at the front, all three being in the same battalion of the Northumberland Fusiliers.

The Dunglinson brothers were among the very first to volunteer to join the 16th (Service) Battalion, 'the Newcastle Battalion', known to most, with affection, as simply 'the Commercials.' The body of Cpl Dan Dunglinson has never been found and he is named on the Thiepval Memorial to the Missing on the Somme. He was twenty-six years old. His older brother, William, gained a commission and died serving with 1st Battalion, Northumberland Fusiliers, on 21 August 1918, less than three months before Armistice Day.

The Indomitable Spirit...

The account of the 18th (Service) Battalion, Northumberland Fusiliers (Tyneside Pioneers), who held the 'Glory Hole' between the advancing lines of the Tyneside Scottish and Tyneside Irish on the first day of the Somme and remained there several days after, wrote their monthly progress report for the regimental journal *St George's Gazette* for July 1916 as follows:

B.E.F. 24 July 1916

I was sorry to miss sending a contribution last month but we were in a ditch awaiting the going down of the flag for the Great Adventure which started on the 1st. It was pleasant and the close of the first phase of the adventure, to find the whole of the Heavy Trench Mortar Detachments present and smiling in spite of the persistent attempts of the enemy to do them down. The shell craters all round their emplacements showed that the cover we had provided for them had been very necessary. Of our doings from the 1st to the 6th, I will only say that we witnessed the advance with pride and envy. Every wave dressed accurately, moving forward steadily, waiting when necessary to correct the alignment, then moving on again without a waver.

Our task was to open up communication with the German front line and keep the detachments of our troops which established themselves at various points in the enemy's trenches supplied with food, water, S.A.A. and BOMBS, and BOMBS and MORE BOMBS!

We came through the action very easily as regards casualties, only 101 of all ranks and 10 of these are doing duty still. Our killed totalled 14, including Lieut. H.W. Coombs, a smart and popular officer. Lieuts. Wood, Helsby and Robson and 2nd Lieuts Nicholson and Cook were wounded but we are glad to hear that they are all doing well, though poor Woods seems to have managed to pick up enough wounds for a platoon but by judging by his letters he is still merry and bright.

Sergeants of the 18th (Service) Battalion, Northumberland Fusiliers (Tyneside Pioneers), 'Somewhere in France', 1916.

5

THE NIGHT THE ZEPPELIN CAME

The First Zeppelin Air Raid on Northumberland, 14 April 1915

Zeppelins were a terror weapon that had caused widespread concern and fear in the public mind over the years immediately before the outbreak of the First World War. The press published diagrams explaining how these huge 'aerial monsters' worked (they were over 150 metres long) and diagrams to demonstrate that Britain was in the range of Zeppelins if they were to be used in an offensive role as bombers.

One of the lingering questions is: did the Zeppelins fly over Britain on reconnaissance flights before the First World War? Reliable witnesses claimed to have seen huge black shadows and the lights of mysterious aircraft described in the press as 'scareships' in the night skies over Britain as early as 1909 and again in 1913. *The Illustrated Chronicle* of 21 October 1914 reported a mysterious light over Blyth in a report entitled 'Was it a Zeppelin?':

It was first seen shortly after eight o'clock and for nearly quarter of an hour lights were exhibited at intervals of three to ten minutes. Almost the entire population of the town turned into the streets to see what they could of the mysterious visitor and the general opinion was that the light was being carried by some type of aircraft.

The night was dark, with only a few stars visible and the flying machine was far too high to enable one to ascertain whether it was of the aeroplane or airship type. One thing, however, was certain, it hung about the vicinity of the town for over half an hour and apparently manoeuvred in a circle. People were curious and strained their eyes and craned their necks in endeavours to elucidate the mystery, while many cracked jokes regarding the threatened Zeppelin from Germany.

The first Zeppelin attack on British soil was carried out by the Zeppelins *L3* and *L4* upon locations along the Norfolk coast on 19 January 1915. The raid was damned in the British and international press as an outrage. An aircraft bombed Colchester, Essex, on 21 February 1915, but the loss of Zeppelins *L3* and the *L4* in snowstorms and foul weather off the Jutland coast in early February, and further bad weather conditions, saw the skies remain clear of Zeppelins over Britain until 14 April 1915.

The secret report compiled from military and police reports and official sources by the Intelligence Section, General Headquarters, Great Britain, states:

L.9 commanded by Kapitän-Leutnant Heinrich Mathy, had meanwhile made several successful reconnaissance flights from North Germany over the North Sea. Her commander was a man of great courage and resource and soon proved himself capable of raiding England with effect. On the night of 14 April he inaugurated the series of raid on Northern England which were to become a speciality of the naval airship service. He is said on this occasion to have first taken his ship up the coast to Jutland to the neighbourhood of Norway, then to have crossed the North Sea to the coast of Scotland and then came southward in order to attack the industrial establishments of the Tyne, which he found with success, though the raid did little damage.

On the night of 14 April 1915 England lay between two anticyclonic systems centred over the Atlantic and Scandinavia respectively. The barometer on the N.E. coast stood at 30.12 inches, rising slowly. There was practically no wind but slight rain or mist over the mouth of the Tyne at the time of the raid. Weather over the North Sea was inclined to be foggy, the night was very dark.

Kptlt Heinrich Mathy, Imperial German Naval Air Service commander of the Zeppelin L.9 that conducted the raid on Northumberland on 14 April 1915.

Multi-view postcard produced to mark the Zeppelin raid on Blyth 14 April 1915.

Mathy appeared off the mouth of the Tyne and coasted as far as Blyth, where she was off the harbour at 7.30 p.m. The Zeppelin appeared to take her bearings then proceeded up the River Blyth to Cambois where she was fired at by infantry [members of C. Company, 1st Northern Cyclist Battalion]. She then went to West Sleekburn, where the first bomb, of incendiary type, was dropped in a field, doing no damage. The airship passed on by Bomarsund and Barrington collieries to Choppington. Four incendiary bombs were dropped on fields on the way. A sixth incendiary bomb was dropped in front of a house at Choppington, breaking a window of the Station Hotel, just before 8.00 p.m. The next bomb thrown was a High Explosive (H.E.) that dropped in a field west of Glebe Farm, Choppington. Two more H.E. bombs were dropped in the same field. The tenth bomb, also H.E., was dropped in a field west of Bedlington, followed by another H.E. in a second field close by. At Bedlington L.9 turned south passing over Crowhall Farm, where a 50 kg H.E. bomb was dropped again in fields doing no damage, though it fell within thirty feet of two police officers [Sgt Marshall and PC Middlemiss], who were saved by throwing themselves flat on the ground.

The Zeppelin then proceeded towards Cramlington, dropping another H.E. bomb in a field, which again did no damage. On Cramlington an incendiary bomb was thrown, which fell through the roof of a building used by the local Urban District Council as a warehouse. A small fire was caused but was soon extinguished by some workmen.

Proceeding south L.9 dropped an incendiary bomb which fell in a field near West Cramlington. The Zeppelin was then seen about two miles south of the latter place, apparently hovering in the air for a short time. Three more incendiary bombs were dropped in this vicinity, falling in a field west of the railway and close to the line. L.9 then turned westward to Seaton Burn and on the way another incendiary bomb fell in the village but caused no damage. The Zeppelin then turned westward in the direction of Dinnington Colliery, a mile distant from

Seaton Burn and when about two-thirds of the distance had been covered a H.E. bomb was dropped in a field, making a large crater. Going thence S.E. the airship passed over Forest Hall at 8.35 p.m. and then went south over Benton, where an incendiary bomb was dropped, falling in a field a little west of the railway station.

The scene of where an incendiary bomb had been dropped by the raiding Zeppelin on Choppington, 14 April 1915.

One of the Zeppelin bomb craters at Bedlington with a fine turnout of curious locals on the morning of 14 April 1915.

ZEPPELIN RAID, APRIL 14th, 1915.
Damaged Building at Cramlington.   (Z3)

The council store building that suffered a bomb dropping through the roof at Cramlington during the Zeppelin raid 14 April 1915.

L.9 then dropped six incendiary bombs at Wallsend. Three did no damage, the fourth went through the roof of a cottage and slightly injured a woman and a little girl (the woman was sitting at the fireside washing the girl and they both had their hair singed, the bomb setting the floor on fire); the fifth and sixth set fire to railway sleepers. An H.E. bomb then fell into the River Tyne between the Electric Power Station and Castner and Kellner's Works, the force of the explosion damaging windows at both places. The last bomb, an incendiary, fell at Hebburn Quay, on the south side of the river, at 8.48 p.m. It struck the concrete floor of a dry dock doing no damage. The Zeppelin then went out to sea at Marsden, between Sunderland and South Shields. She was pursued by two aeroplanes that ascended from Cramlington but the pilots could see nothing of her. Her height is said never to have exceeded 2,000 feet but this is probably an under-estimate.

The H.E. bombs were all estimated to be around 50 kg in weight. The monetary value of the damage caused by the raid was estimated at £55.

Few people realise that wherever a bomb falls it becomes a crime scene. Some of the original reports still survive and Superintendent James Irving of Blyth Police Office wrote a report to his Chief Constable, Fullarton James, at the County Police Office, Morpeth, which provides us with a first-hand view of the first ever bombing raid on Northumberland by one who was there. Dated 15 April 1915, it states,

Sir,

I beg to report that a Zeppelin Airship appeared at the mouth of the Harbour at 7.30 p.m. last night. I was in the Market Place and on seeing it I got soldiers and Special Constables to put the town in darkness. This was done in few minutes and the Gas and the Electricity turned off at its source.

Detective Andrews was despatched to Whitley Bay and Special Constable Young to Bedlington to warn all concerned, the telephone being impossible. The Airship appeared to take its bearings and proceeded up the river, swerving inwards to the Market Place, then across to Cambois and then to West Sleekburn, Barrington Colliery, Choppington Station, Glebe Farm, Bedlington Cemetery, Lane End Farm and south of Hartford Hall to Plessey Checks.

Bombs were dropped as follows:

No. 1 dropped in a field immediately to the West of Sleekburn, found by PC Carr at 1.00 a.m. this morning. Made a circular hole about 1 foot by 2 feet deep, fell vertically, no damage to property. This was an incendiary bomb.

No. 2 in a field east of Bomarsund Colliery, made a similar hole, no damage, said to have been taken away by a soldier, also incendiary.

No. 3 Incendiary bomb fell in a field west of Bomarsund Colliery, no damage. Found by James Arris of 3 Red Row, Barrington, at 5.00 a.m. on 15th April. Similar hole to above.

No. 4 Incendiary bomb fell in Brick Field east of Barrington Colliery, found by James Arris at 8.30 p.m. on 14th, no damage, similar cavity formed.

No. 5 Incendiary bomb dropped in Brick Field east of highway and south of Railway Station at Choppington, no damage, similar cavity, found by Thomas Smith, Office Row, Barrington, at 8.30 p.m. on 14th inst.

No. 6 Incendiary bomb dropped in a hedge in front of German House, Choppington. Station Hotel windows broken, similar cavity to others, found by John Charlton, 6, Office Row, Barrington about 8.10 p.m., on 14th inst.

No. 7 Explosive bomb dropped in a field west of Glebe Farm, Choppington, parallel and adjoining Netherton Old Waggon Way. Caused a crater 6ft by 2½ft. deep, no other damage. A portion of the bomb found by Sergeant Ernest Graham, Bedlington at 6.00 a.m. on 15th inst.

No. 8 same field, details similar to No 7 but not portion found.

No. 9 same field as Nos 7 & 8, no portion found details similar

No. 10 also Explosive, dropped in a field 500 yards west of Bedlington Police Station, formed crater 12ft diameter by 3 feet deep. 3 windows broken in Catholic Row, Bedlington. No portion found.

No. 11 Incendiary Bomb dropped in same field as No. 12, no damage, similar cavity to similar bombs. No portion recovered.

No. 12 also Explosive dropped in a field south of Lane House Farm, Bedlington, crater 10ft by 2¾ft deep, 4 small panes of glass broken at farm. No portion found.

All appear to have fallen vertically. A man alleged that he was injured at Hirst Head, Bedlington, his hand bring scratched and trousers torn but no credence is placed on his story, other people in the same neighbourhood allege that his injury was caused by a barbed wire fence. This is most probable.

The fragments of bombs Nos. 1, 3, 4, 5, 6, & 7 are at Bedlington Police Station and have been dealt with as per instructions.

There was no panic anywhere, all the Special Constables acted according to previous instructions and many also called at the Police Station, offering services. Each Special Shop Constable at Blyth took charge of his allotted shop until midnight and the Cyclist Corps were in readiness. The Motor Controls previously arranged were worked and no unknown cars or suspicious circumstances were noted in any part of the Division.

All constables were on duty.

The *Illustrated Chronicle* of Friday 16 April highlights the narrowest escapes from death during the air raid:

The Germans dropped two bombs at the high end of Station Road, Wallsend. One fell in the roadway and made a hole and the other fell through the roof of the house, 238, Station Road, occupied by Mr. G. Robinson, a blacksmith at Messrs. Swan, Hunter and Wigram Richardson Ltd., his wife, two children and Miss May Taylor, a friend.

In the roof of the house there is a hole where the slates had been knocked out. The attic and its contents are badly burned. In the attic floor there is another hole and in the room beneath, where the ceiling fell, other damage has been done. Mrs Robinson related her experience to our representative and there is no doubt that both she and Miss Taylor acted very bravely under trying circumstances. Mrs Robinson was engaged in bathing her little girl, aged three years, in the kitchen under the attic. Miss Taylor and Mrs Robison's little boy aged 7 were also in the room. A sudden and loud explosion occurred and the ceiling came down on to Mrs. Robinson and her companion.

Some burning liquid fell and set fire to Mrs. Robinson's hair and also to the hair of the little boy. The room immediately took fire. The two women at once rushed out by the back with the children, a few doors away. They then pluckily returned to the burning house and Mrs. Robinson rushed through the flames and turned off the gas at the meter.

Keeping a brave face on it: the wife and children left behind by Durham Light Infantry soldier. Many brave young men volunteered for war but many of those who enlisted in the north were older men in their late twenties and thirties with young families.

6

HOME FIRES BURNING

Going away to training camps ready for war was surrounded with a patriotic atmosphere of cheering crowds, waving flags and 'a good send-off' by family and friends, but those who marched away to 'do their bit' left huge gaps in the families and communities they left behind. In many instances siblings wanted to serve together, such as brothers Jack, Ralph, Jim and Frank Hankin who all joined the Tyneside Scottish, or George, William, Edward, Robert and James Bateman, both

Mr Sidney Gamblin of Gateshead (second from the right) and three of his sons, all of them serving in 9th Battalion, Durham Light Infantry (T.F.), 1915.

sets of brothers from Blyth. There were also the five sons of Samuel Owens and the six Thain brothers of Ashington, or the five sons of William Walton, the foreman of the Newcastle Water Co. of Grey Street, Newcastle. Indeed, there were regular features in local newspapers on families and extended families from all across Tyneside who had all of their sons join up, but you would have to go a long way to surpass Mr and Mrs S. Purvis of Addison near Blaydon who had eight sons, one adopted son and one son-in-law serving in the land forces.

The sense of loss of young men from local society was felt most profoundly in the smaller, more rural communities of Northumberland. A typical story was that of Bilton Bank, Lesbury, a mining community consisting of a row of twenty or thirty dwellings around 3 ½ miles south-east of Alnwick. Every one of the homes in the row had at least one member of the household enlisted. Some had two sons away, and others three, but the end house of the row held the record – Mr and Mrs Robert Baxter had five sons serving with the Colours. In an interview with a local newspaper Mrs Baxter's comments reveal some of the thoughts and feelings of many mothers at the time:

"Yes," said Mrs Baxter to me, "I am proud of my boys. I have a right to be, but one cannot take that sad feeling away from a mother's heart when her boys are gone from her. "I am proud" repeats Mrs Baxter, "but only in a way. I would sooner have the lads with me here; then I would know they were safe from harm. Had one or two gone it would not have been so bad but the whole five going away makes the home dreadfully lonely and quiet."

Then Mrs Baxter proceeded to look for the photographs of her sons. "This one," she explained, "is a portrait of my eldest son Tom. He is thirty-nine years old and is serving in the Guards. He is married, and has left a wife and one child behind him. "Next to Thomas" she proceeds, "comes John, aged twenty-eight years. John is in the 2nd Battalion, Northumberland Fusiliers, Machine Gun Section, Subathu, India. "I know he is anxious to go to the front" said the mother sadly, "for the last letter I had from him he said: I am just wishing to get to the war. You may think it horrible to take human lives but if I get the chance I'll be off like a shot and he's just the likely lad to do his best in the fighting line." She continued. The three younger boys, Robert aged twenty-four, James aged twenty-three and David aged twenty-one, are in the 7th Battalion, Northumberland Fusiliers, the youngest one being stationed at Blyth, and the other two at Gosforth Park, Newcastle.

"Out of Shilbottle alone one hundred men have gone to serve their King and country. We are all proud of them. It can never be said that Bilton Banks has not done their duty. We womenfolk are proud of our husbands and sons, and we pray that they will all come back safely. Besides having five sons away at the front," said Mrs Baxter, "I have also a grandson, William Smith, and he is only fifteen years old. He has gone out as a little drummer boy, so that makes the total up to six.

A remarkable recruiting record was also held by Kitty Brewster, near Blyth. The village comprised around sixty-six houses, and out of the sixty males who are eligible for enlistment no fewer than fifty-six (96 per cent) enlisted, leaving just twelve men who were too old to enlist but who declared that, should they be needed, to a man they were also willing to 'do their bit' if they were to be called.

Women Did their Bit Too!

One of the most important organisations that provided so much for troops both at home and abroad was the Young Men's Christian Association (YMCA). Based in extant buildings in towns where there was a significant military presence (where they also provided hostels), in tents or wooden prefabricated buildings their 'huts' provided canteens with books to read, writing paper and envelopes free of charge, and stamps, hot drinks and snacks for reasonable prices.

The YMCA was mostly run by volunteers: there were male staff who were over military service age or below the medical requirements for active service but for the most part the canteens were staffed by women. Some of those stalwart local ladies who went abroad with 'the canteens' were Miss Kate Richardson, Miss Mary Hogg, Miss Gladys Munby and Miss Winnie Tindle, who went out to France to staff the YMCA hut presented by the Borough of Tynemouth in 1916, and there was a waiting list of ladies to rotate tours of duty with them.

Soldiers on leave in Newcastle were always grateful for the YMCA Naval & Military Hostel, 1916.

The YMCA Hut on Half Moon Lane, Gateshead, shortly after its opening by Lady Jellicoe in March 1916.

Closer to home the YMCA set up a canteen at the Central Station and there was a naval and military hostel opened by Lady Jellicoe (wife of Admiral of the Fleet Sir John Jellicoe) on Fenkel Street, near the old Assembly Rooms, Newcastle, in March 1916, which provided accommodation, refreshments and entertainments for thousands of soldiers and sailors that passed through Newcastle during the war. Lady Jellicoe also opened another commodious YMCA centre on Half Moon Lane, Gateshead, on the same day.

In 1916 it was reported there were fifty-three YMCA centres in Northumberland and Durham in the summertime and twenty-three in the winter, eleven of which were the famous YMCA wooden 'huts'. These were no small affair though, usually 80 feet long and 72 feet wide, and each hut was divided in such a way that there were enough beds to sleep 100 and a concert room (with stage), a large recreation room and a writing room with refreshment bar. The premises also included a kitchen, lavatories and stores. A bed on the floor would cost 6d a night, a cubicle and bed 1s or, if the 'accommodation was too much taxed', a charge of 4d would be made for men to use the floor with three blankets. For an additional 3d a man could also have a bath.

There were 'huts' at a number of the local Army camps like Alnwick, Cramlington, Whitley Bay and Gosforth. During the war if camps changed and huts became redundant they were not left to rot and they would be redeployed, such as when the military left Gosforth Camp the 'hut' was redeployed to Consett.

The Young Women's Christian Association (YWCA) also played their part. When the pressure of munitions work called for the provision of special accommodation for women and girls, a building was opened at Elswick. The scheme proved such a success that it was proposed that another place should be opened nearer the city centre where girls in lodgings could form a club 'at which they might spend enjoyable evenings', thus the YWCA Girl's Club was created on the Cross House site, Westgate Road, opened by the Dowager Marchioness of Londonderry in March 1916.

Comforts for troops in the trenches available from Boots in 1915.

A Comforting Thought...

Wor lads at the front were never forgotten. Communities, be they village, town or city, sent comforts to those serving their king and country. It's often imagined these schemes were just for Christmas but the comforts committees kept their local servicemen as well supplied as they could and that included those who were prisoners of war. Most of the comfort groups were run by women and had great teams of women workers sourcing the items to send through public appeals or making them by sewing or knitting. Typical among them was the Newcastle Commercial Battalions Ladies Committee, who had a weekly working party that met at the Connaught Hall. Their chair was Kate Eeles whose letter of thanks published in the press in July 1916 gives a small hint of how many kind contributions such organisations received on a regular bases:

Advert for blanket cloth waistcoats available from Dunn & Co, Market Street and Grey Street, Newcastle. Comforts from home, whether purchased or made by the many sewing and knitting groups, were always appreciated by the boys at the front.

We are very grateful to the following ladies for gifts received:

Mrs Renwick, Morpeth, 10 pairs socks; Mrs V. Thompson, 1, Tankerville Terrace, 1 pair socks; Mrs. Ritson, Muggleswick, 3 pairs socks; Mrs Harrison, Eslington Lodge, 2 pairs socks; Mrs Newbiggin, 17, Tankerville Terrace, 1 pair socks; Mrs J. G. Angus, Westover, Low Fell, 1 pair socks; Mrs Berwis, 3 pairs socks; Mrs Stephens, Ravenstone, Corbridge, 20 pairs socks; Mrs J. S. Clark, Rosedale, Gosforth, 12 pairs socks; Miss Harper, 24, The Grove, Gosforth, 3 pairs socks; Mrs Joicey, Warkworth, 2 pairs socks; Mrs Pybus, Kildale, Gosforth, 4 pairs socks; Miss E, Walton, 2 Osborne Road, 1 pair socks.

The many thousands of socks that have been sent to the Front have been of the greatest benefit to the men, and the committee beg to return their sincere thanks to all the kind contributors who have worked so hard to attain the splendid result. Wool can be procured during August from the following: Mrs. Renwick, Springhill, Morpeth; Mrs. Lunn, Heathfield, Gateshead; Mrs. Hunter, Roath House, Low Fell; and Mrs. Laws, 15, Tenth Avenue, Heaton. Parcels can be left at the Connaught Hall.

It was not just the Army who benefitted either; the boys at sea also received comforts parcels. One of the earliest schemes began in October 1914 with an appeal in the local press for comforts for the crews of Tyneside Depot minesweepers. The wording was absolutely typical of the tenor of appeals at the time: 'Some 6,000 brave men are engaged in sweeping the seas to rid us of the mines which are such a menace to our shipping and the shipping of neutral powers. The dastardly way in which these instruments of destruction have been strewn about the North Sea makes it incumbent upon us to see that those who are engaged in clearing them away should have their comfort well looked after.' Donations either in goods made or money were requested to provide the following for each seaman: 'One jersey (dark blue), one muffler, one Balaclava helmet, one pair of long mittens, one pair of fishermen's stockings, two pairs of socks, one pair (woven) pants, one vest, one quarter pound packet of shag tobacco.' All donations were to be sent to the town hall marked 'Mine Sweepers' Garments'.

The ladies of the Soldiers and Sailors Comforts Working Group, Blaydon, 1914.

The Help the Wounded fundraising event at Warkworth, 26 August 1915

Events to raise money to support local auxiliary war hospitals and hospital comforts funds for British and allied troops began within days of the outbreak of the war. Among the first in the country was the 'Newcastle, Tyneside and District Ladies' Society for Aid to Hospitals During the War' led by Newcastle Mayor Norah Johnstone Wallace (wife of Lord Mayor Johnstone Wallace 1913–14), who by 12 August 1914 could announce they had established a Central Committee Working Centre at the Friend's Meeting House on Pilgrim Street, Newcastle, and further working centres at Jesmond, East End, West End, Gosforth, Riding Mill, Corbridge, Newburn, Throckley and Westerhope. Similar groups could also be found all along Tyneside, but as the war progressed the demand for bandages outstripped the supplies offered by surgical firms and the prices they charged became an issue, so bandage parties were created. Prominent among them was the Scotswood and Elswick Bandage Party that had Lady Lunn (wife of Lord Mayor Sir George Lunn, who served no less than three terms during the First World War 1915–17) as their president. The party itself was organised by Miss M. and Miss V. Crosbie, who drew together a party of workers, mainly composed of teachers, from Newcastle. They were given rooms free of charge by the Director of Education and Messrs Singer loaned sewing machines. The party met on five evenings every week and they skilfully set to work making bandages and dressings in flannelette, calico, butter muslin and even supplied them embedded with sphagnum moss. Every local hospital was supplied with bandages and in France, British and French war hospitals were sent extra supplies of bandages when required. Between January 1916 and January 1919 the Elswick and Scotswood Bandage Party despatched 70,523 bandages.

A lapel badge worn by the volunteer workers of the Elswick and Scotswood Bandage Party that supplied over 70,000 bandages to local war hospitals as well as British and French military hospitals in France.

A postcard tribute to Britain's War Workers postcard with the Newcastle lady window cleaners (centre) and a local postwoman on the right, 1915.

Women at Work

The War Office provided the wives or dependant mothers of servicemen with a separation allowance but it has never been easy for a mum to bring up a family of children on her own. In many cases extended family and neighbours helped by looking after the young children. It was the patriotic thing to do because this meant many women were able to take up their chance to 'do their bit' and do something the likes of which many married women had not done before the war – they went out to work. They took jobs in shops, offices and telephone exchanges in unprecedented numbers, worked trade carts from milk rounds to window cleaning, became postwomen, toiled on the land, worked on public transport and, above all, entered the factories to work on munitions or did their bit in the shipyards.

The term 'munitions' did not just refer to the manufacture of shells but a whole host of operations as diverse as pulling flax crops to manufacturing wooden boxes for military purposes, and even working in the various stages of aircraft manufacture – broadly speaking, if it involved 'feeding the guns' of the war effort it could be titled munitions work – so a girl could have been involved in munitions throughout the war and never touch a gun shell!

A fine group of Newcastle Munitionettes in their overalls, 1916. Many of them proudly wear their triangular 'On War Service' badges and a variety of sweetheart and patriotic brooches at the necks of their blouses.

In her article 'Women's Work in Engineering and Shipbuilding during the War' (the *Shipbuilder*, 1919), the Hon. Lady Parsons pointed out that by 1918 90 per cent of the workers in munitions were women and continued:

Some of the more skilled work that women learned to do requires emphasis because there is a strong tendency among engineers to consider that women are only capable of doing repetition work on fool-proof machines. There is no doubt that many women developed great mechanical skill and a real love of their work.

Both precision work and labour-intensive machining on lathes were carried out by women to great success in the Elswick's ordnance works; they worked in the woodworking department on frames and canvas at the Armstrong-Whitworth aircraft factory in the old Town Moor Skating Rink, and the women painters and acetylene welders established a good reputation for themselves in the shipyards of the Tyne from early on in the war. With so many men leaving the shipyards to serve in the military in 1914, the women war workers were most certainly needed and they certainly had their work cut out for them. The total output of ships of all kinds from the Tyne, Wear and Tees during the war amounted to 1,130 vessels of all sizes and descriptions with a tonnage of 3,324,912. Taking the duration of the war as 221 weeks, it would mean an average of five ships a week were delivered.

On the Tyne companies such as Armstrong-Whitworth; Hawthore, Leslie, Palmers, and Swan Hunter & Wigham Richardson were all connected with the construction of battleships, but it was Swan Hunter who delivered the largest number of ships – 126 of them. There were also a number of companies who made considerable numbers of marine engines, such as Parsons Marine Steam Turbine Co., and the first parent ship for seaplanes, the *Ark Royal*, was also built locally by the Blyth Shipbuilding and Dry Docks Co.

So, who were the munitions girls? Although there was a greater mix of classes 'mucking in' to help along the Tyne, 'nice' girls from middle-class and upper-class families tended to be guided towards nursing organizations or women's services, and the munitions girls were predominantly from domestic-service backgrounds with a liberal smattering of shop assistants, laundry workers, clerks and similar working- and lower-middle-class occupations. Requirements were similar to any other occupation in this employment sector – basic education and the physical fitness to do the job was enough. The days were long, many factories working twenty-four hours a day with girls working twelve-hour shifts, typically 6 a.m. to 6 p.m. and vice versa for the next shift. Hard work and long hours, and they were not well paid. There were great disputes over the inequality of wages; men were paid an average £4 6*s* 6*d* whereas women only received £2 2*s* 4*s*, but most girls were quite happy because the wages were higher than they were accustomed to before the war.

The girls would be expected to come to work in 'working clothes' but would be typically issued a pair of wooden-soled clogs (sparks caused by metal segs, studded or even plain leather-soled boots are not a good idea when working with explosives). In the most critical areas the girls wore fabric slippers or even rubber gumboots. All would be issued the relevant pattern of 'National Shell Overall', which comprised a drawstring or elasticated cap and a flame-retardant canvas or cotton-twill overall with a belted waist.

Badges, originally of the button hole type, were issued to the workers with an entitlement card that had to be carried at all times along with their general issue identity cards to show the worker was entitled to be in the factory and to show they were 'On War Service' if they were challenged by someone asking why were they not 'doing their bit' in uniform. Initially many of the factories not owned by the Ministry of Munitions made their own identity badges but by 1915 the officially issued 'On War Service' badges were standard, and the triangular 'On War Service' badge with the pin back suitable for both men and women issued in 1916 was soon adopted as the badge of the women war workers proud to be affectionately known as Munitionettes.

The dangers many of these girls were exposed to were very real. Stringent precautions were enforced to safeguard against sparks or employees having a crafty smoke in areas where gunpowder or cordite were involved. Another danger was from overexposure to the chemicals in cordite and especially TNT, which could turn hair a ginger colour and skin yellow – hence the girls became nicknamed 'canaries'. Despite warnings from doctors, girls kept on working and, after a few serious illnesses and fatalities, it became common policy to send batches of the 'canaries' off to coastal resorts to take the air and clear out their systems.

Because of the nature of work and requirement of mobility, especially in the shipyards, the shell overall outfit was soon supplemented with trousers, something no young lady would have been seen wearing on the street before the war. This additional item of clothing was worn as a badge of honour on the street by the munitions girls. In this same spirit of freedom female munitions workers started to wear a little make-up and even ventured into pubs unaccompanied by men, and in the interests of keeping fit and getting clean, healthy air into the lungs of the girls, they were encouraged to take up an outdoor sport unheard of for women before the war – football!

The first football cup for women came into existence during the First World War and was popularly known as the Munitionettes' Cup. Competed for by female munition workers' teams in north-east England, it was officially titled the Tyne Wear & Tees Alfred Wood Munition Girls Cup. The first winners of the trophy were Blyth Spartans, who defeated Bolckow Vaughan 5–0 in a replayed final tie at Middlesbrough on 18 May 1918.

With the end of the First World War came the end of the need for most of the munitions girls, but they had changed society's attitude to women in so many ways and played a major role in earning women the right to vote.

Munitionettes and male staff at a Newcastle works, *c.* 1917. This photograph gives some idea of the scale of the female workforce taken on by the engineering firms of the area during the First World War.

George V and Queen Mary talking to some of the female shipyard workers during their official visit to the shipyards of the Tees and Tyneside, June 1917. (Newcastle Library)

The 1st Northern General Hospital RAMC (T.F.), Armstrong College, Newcastle, 1914.

War Hospitals

Over the years immediately before 1914 the War Office had recognised that in the event of a major European war the existing medical arrangements for Britain's armed forces would be wholly inadequate. Some form of supplementary aid would be required in addition to the Territorial Force Medical Service to supply and equip auxiliary war hospitals and provide care for the thousands of casualties that could be returned from a British Expeditionary Force fighting on the Continent. After the creation of the Territorial Force in 1908, the War Office issued its Scheme for the Organisation of Voluntary Aid in England and Wales the following year.

The British Red Cross Society and Order of St John (although at that time working as separate voluntary aid societies) began to establish its first so-called Voluntary Aid Detachments (VADs) to recruit and train local volunteers, both male and female, for the task. The scheme went well and was promoted and expanded in 1912.

To become full and proficient members of their Voluntary Aid Detachment, girls were expected to train for and pass examinations in both first aid and nursing. The male detachments trained in first aid only, and in war they served mostly in corps responsible for the transport of the wounded, setting up and furnishing the auxiliary war hospitals and acting as ward orderlies, but the VAD (a term applied to all serving in the VAD system, but more especially to the nurses) were to 'regard himself or herself as part of the Medical Organisation of the Territorial Force, available to serve in the event of war'.

By August 1914 thousands had already volunteered and trained across the country, and there were already sixty-five Voluntary Aid Detachments in Northumberland and Durham and more would soon follow. Working with the Newcastle detachments of the Church Nursing and Ambulance Brigade, they also established a Military Rest Station at the Central Railway Station just three days after the outbreak of war that was staffed round the clock by rotas of trained volunteers until 31 August, when it was taken over entirely by VADs.

VA Detachments and single members could volunteer to be 'mobile', meaning they were willing to serve outside their home county and even abroad if required. Both counties supplied detachments and personnel for duty both at home and abroad. It is noteworthy that No. VI (Northern) District St John Ambulance Brigade hold the honour of having furnished the first Voluntary Aid Detachment to be called up for war service in the First World War. VAD nurses served all over the world and whole detachments of volunteers were sent from Tyneside to the likes of the base hospitals at Rouen and Boulogne to assist with the wounded or to become orderlies and workers at some of Britain's biggest military hospitals, like Netley, near Southampton. The Northumberland and Durham VA Detachments also helped form the original staff of the first hospital train to be run under the Joint Committee of the British Red Cross Society and St John Ambulance.

The War Office requisitioned Armstrong College and its adjoining buildings on the outbreak of war for use as 1st Northern General Hospital. It would be staffed by Royal Army Medical Corps (RAMC) personnel and military nurses from the Territorial Force Nursing Service with a capacity for 104 officers and 1,420 wounded soldiers.

An additional 200 beds were claimed for military patients at the Royal Victoria Infirmary and the pair worked closely together for the duration of the war. The RVI also provided a month's training for VAD nurses before they took up their formal rotas to supplement the qualified nursing staff in the hospitals.

Military and house medical staff, territorial and qualified nurses with VAD nurses of the 1st Northern General Hospital, *c.* 1917.

The first ambulance train carrying 111 wounded soldiers from the front arrived at Platform 8, Newcastle Central Station, from Southampton on 15 September 1914. The platform was entirely cleared and, shortly after 6.00 p.m., a long procession of eighty motorcars came onto the platform followed by the RAMC and St John Ambulance Brigade carrying stretchers, nurses, officers, and, lastly, Lt-Gen. Sir Herbert Plumer, Commander-in-Chief, Northern Command.

Despite the authorities trying to keep the arrival secret in case a crowd impeded the work of the medical services meeting the soldiers, a considerable number of people came to the station and the arrival of the train was anxiously awaited. Exactly at 6.30 p.m. the train steamed alongside the platform and several 'Tommies' were seen to be looking out of the windows as it pulled in and answering the cheers of those who were privileged to witness the scene.

The *Illustrated Chronicle* picks up the story:

Then for over an hour and a half, came a sorrowful procession, brightened only by the apparent good spirits of the soldiers, who, despite their wounds – many of them of a serious nature – smiled their appreciation of the reception, which was at once cordial and sympathetic. There were several ambulance transports waiting in the portico, and the more serious cases were carried to these. The first soldier to be carried out had an injury to his leg. He looked ill, but raising himself on his elbow when he heard the cheering, he waved his greetings to the people. Other men, with the greatest sangfroid, puffed at their pipes and cigarettes, and there were many who were so ill they could not take an interest in the proceedings. Having attended to the serious cases, the remainder, with bandaged arms and heads, hopped into motor-cars and were quickly driven away to hospital. These men laughed and talked with their attendants and, when someone in the crowd shouted 'Are we down-hearted?' they answered with a full throated 'No!'

The casualties were soldiers from a variety of regiments, from Highlanders to artillerymen, and had received gunshot wounds, chiefly in the shoulder, body and legs. With the careful and sympathetic handling of the medical personnel present, they were transferred to the Royal Victoria Infirmary and the Military Hospital at Armstrong College.

As the numbers of returned sick and wounded from the battlefields increased, the pressure was on to create more hospital beds, so early in 1915 the War Office introduced a scheme to evacuate the patients of extant county asylums for the mentally ill to other, smaller facilities and convert the largest premises into war hospitals.

In February 1915 Newcastle City Council were informed that the War Office required the Newcastle City Asylum at Coxlodge, and its patients were removed to other asylums in Northumberland and adjoining counties. The premises were refitted and renamed the Northumberland War Hospital with accommodation for 1,040 patients, with the first convoy of wounded soldiers arriving there on 29 May 1915. To give some idea of the scale of numbers involved, the ambulance trains bringing wounded to the Northumberland War Hospital arrived at West Gosforth Station at least once a week during the heaviest fighting periods of the war, and by 1917 it was reckoned the St John Ambulance men of Newcastle and Gateshead, all of them unpaid volunteers, had helped convey around 20,000 cases from the station to the hospital.

The military also took over the Workhouse Hospital and some of the other buildings at Brighton Grove to become an 800-bed facility for the treatment of venereal diseases in soldiers. The Walkergate Hospital took on soldiers with infectious diseases and treated them in pavilions after initial concerns over available space. The married quarters at Fenham Barracks were converted to a hospital,

The Northumberland War Hospital, Gosforth, 1915.

Some of the RAMC officers, nurses and orderlies of the Northumberland War Hospital, *c.* 1916.

there was a brigade hospital set up at Condercum House, Benwell, and the 2/3 Northumbrian Field Ambulance Hospitals were established in former private residences at No. 41 and No. 43 Jesmond Road, Newcastle.

There were also pre-war convalescent hospitals for consumptives or the likes of the St Mary Magdalene Home for Incurables that offered its Richardson Wing of forty beds from the outbreak of war and received its first patients in December 1914. It became a convalescent wing for soldiers drafted from the 1st Northern General Hospital. Under the redoubtable Matron Miss Ethel Wilkes, her staff, military nurses and volunteers from the Red Cross, the wing cared for hundreds of soldiers over the duration of the war, many of them recovering from serious operations and wounds.

There were also privately financed hospitals sponsored by religious groups or rich benefactors 'for the duration' of the war, such as the hospital established at Linden Hall by sisters Muriel and Eve Adamson, the daughters of Colonel John Adamson, the owner. The larger military hospitals were also supported by an array of temporary hospitals like the one in Clara Vale staffed by local ambulance workers and wards established in pavilions and in other nearby buildings when heavy casualty returns required them.

The greatest numbers of auxiliary war hospitals were created under the VAD scheme. Shortly after the outbreak of war public meetings were held to ascertain which public buildings and houses in the village, town or city local to them were available for conversion to Auxiliary War Hospitals. Many families patriotically offered a spare bedroom, and municipal buildings such as schools and concert halls were made available. However, the need to concentrate convalescent servicemen in

Nursing staff and convalescent soldiers outside the Richardson Wing at the St Mary Magdalene Home for Incurables, Newcastle, *c.* 1916.

one place made their dispersal in ones and twos a nuisance, and many municipal buildings were required for their original purpose, even in time of war. In most cases a large local house or the rectory proved to be the most practical place in which to open a hospital, although hospital 'annexes' were opened in public buildings or other houses when returning casualties overwhelmed the bed space available. The British Red Cross Society and the St John Ambulance became a joint war organisation working together, and by the end of 1914 many of the auxiliary war hospitals that they established were often simply referred to as 'Red Cross Hospitals'.

The auxiliary war hospitals established by the British Red Cross Society and Order of St John of Jerusalem in Northumberland 1914–1918 were:

1/ Northumberland V.A., Howick Hall, Lesbury.
2/ Northumberland V.A., Haggerston Castle, Beal
3/ Northumberland V.A., Convalescent Home, Hextol Terrace, Hexham
3/ Northumberland V.A., (Extension), Cotfield, Temperley Place, Hexham
4/ Northumberland V.A., Dilston Hall, Corbridge-on-Tyne
5/ Northumberland V.A., 48, Percy Gardens, Tynemouth
6/ Northumberland V.A., Borough Hall, Wellway, Morpeth
6/ Northumberland V.A., (Extension), Moore House, Whalton
7/ Northumberland V.A., Oxford House, Oxford Street, Whitley Bay
8/ Northumberland V.A., Duchess's School, Bailiffgate, Alnwick (transferred to Alnwick Camp April 1916*)
9/ Northumberland V.A., Chesters House, Humshaugh
10/ Northumberland V.A., Pendower Hall, Newcastle-on-Tyne
11/ Northumberland V.A., Woolsington Camp, Woolsington
12/ Northumberland V.A., Fowberry Towers and Hetton House, Belford
13/ Northumberland V.A., Etal Manor, Cornhill-on-Tweed
14/ Northumberland V.A., Holeyn Hall, Wylam-on-Tyne
15/ Northumberland V.A., Brinkburn High House, Pauperhaugh, S.O.
16/ Northumberland V.A., Ashington Infirmary, Ashington
17/Northumberland V.A., Callaly Castle, Whittingham, R.S.O.

(*This became the Alnwick Military Convalescent Hospital, one of a new breed of military hospitals formed from March 1916 to keep recovering soldiers under military control. Alnwick was for men from Northern and Scottish Commands, those of Scottish descent or serving in Scottish Regiments.)

There was also a St John Ambulance Brigade Hospital at No. 6 Kensington Terrace, Newcastle, and there were more auxiliary war hospitals along the Tyne at Mill Dam, South Shields, Jarrow, Hebburn Hall, Teams, Saltwell Towers at Saltwell Park and notably Whinney House, Gateshead, one of the largest auxiliary hospitals in the north of England. By the end of 1915 the Voluntary Aid Hospitals provided, under the auspices of the Red Cross and St John, well over 1,100 beds and had 4,714 workers engaged in attending to sick and wounded soldiers in Northumberland and Durham.

A ward with nursing staff and patients at one of our local war hospitals, *c.* 1916.

Many of the VA hospitals in the country had a 'family' atmosphere, with the owner of the house or his wife as commandant of the detachment, and VADs drawn from its domestic staff and local girls. The care supplied was directed by a medical officer (often a local doctor) and the superintendent (a trained nurse). In the early years of the war many of these professionals provided their services free of charge, and some did so throughout the war, but payments were allowed, with a medical officer drawing £1 a day, matrons, sisters-in-charge and ward sisters paid one guinea (£1 1s) a week, and staff nurses (with two years' training) £40 a year. The VAD nurses who served part-time in their local hospital were unpaid, but expenses for board and lodging, laundry (up to a limit of 2s 6d) and travel to and from the hospital could be claimed.

The position of VAD nurse was often the reserve of the young ladies from local middle-class families who could afford to give the time, pay for the lectures and had £1 19s 2½d to buy a uniform (although later in the war local VAD units did have funds to issue uniforms, or at least replace worn-out aprons, collars and cuffs). Officially, VAD nursing members had to be twenty-three to thirty-eight years old to serve in military hospitals, but if girls looked old enough and were keen enough they would get in. Girls as young as seventeen became VADs, especially in the local auxiliary war hospitals. They were appointed on two weeks' probation. If found to be suitable, they would be expected to serve for up to three months and many served for much longer. The engagement of VAD members could be terminated if 'at any time they were found unfit in any respect for service'.

To provide twenty-four-hour cover, VADs worked shifts, girls arriving on foot, riding bicycles or being dropped off by pony and cart. Although they may have been assigned certain core duties, no two days would be quite the same for a VAD. Convalescent men were allocated to the hospitals from two sources: some would be dispatched on trains or by ambulance after treatment in the main county or district war hospital, others would come direct from France having passed through continental field hospitals with 'Blighty wounds', which, if they only required basic treatment and convalescence, could mean that men were sent directly to an auxiliary war hospital, many still in their muddy and bloody uniforms.

A telegram would be sent to the auxiliary war hospital commandant to alert her of the arrival of fresh wounded. Ambulances and ambulance cars for non-stretcher cases were soon provided for the Newcastle hospitals by fundraising and generous gifts from clubs and societies, and wealthy individuals. In many outlying towns, however, there were no ambulances and hastily converted delivery vehicles and private cars were used, along with a motley collection of wheelchairs and hand-drawn carriages, with VAD escorts for the walking wounded.

When arriving at the hospital, the male orderlies would assist the storekeeper in exchanging khaki for the flannel 'hospital blue' uniform of jacket and trousers, white shirt and red tie worn with the soldier's own cap and boots for trips out of doors (slippers being issued for inside wear). The soft and shapeless 'blues' aided the identification of any wandering serviceman who'd slipped out, perhaps for a strictly against the rules pint! Times of blues shortages, when there were heavy numbers of returning wounded, can be noted in old photographs when you see convalescent troops still wearing their khaki uniforms while in hospital.

A typical day began with nurses assisting those patients marked 'Up' to rise, shave, wash and dress before breakfast. Some patients would be marked 'Up from and to', the specific times of day set by the medical officer (MO). Patients ordered 'bed rest' would be made to look presentable for the MO's inspection rounds. The nurses would follow the MO, commandant and superintendent during this inspection. Those patients able to stand to attention would snap to it by their beds, the conscious bed-bound lying at attention. Once the MO's rounds were over, the VAD nurses would assist the MO and superintendent in changing dressings. Young VADs were frequently confronted with sights that would haunt their dreams for the rest of their lives.

Throughout the day bedpans and sputum cups had to be supplied and emptied, and Nelson's inhalers used to clear congestion on the lungs. The incapable would be fed, and those learning to walk again helped onto crutches or supported. To occupy convalescent troops most wards had been gifted a host of comforts, such as gramophones, books and magazines. Crafts such as rag rug making and embroidery were taught to the bed-bound. Many VADs patiently helped the wounded to write home, took dictation or read letters to those blinded, always doing their best to remain cheerful. There were regular teas and concerts held at the hospitals to raise the funds to keep them running and help to boost morale. The VADs would help the convalescent troops to make decorations, such as paper link chains and Chinese lanterns. If there was a sports element – like cricket – involved in such an event, the convalescent soldier might bat while a local boy scout, recruited by the nurses, would be the soldier's runner.

An evocative account of a visit to the wounded soldiers at Armstrong College was published in *North Mail* on 5 October 1914:

It brings a lump to the throat to watch the silent gratitude of these brave fellows for the tender ministrations and constant vigilance of the patient 'sisters.' The very contrast of their surroundings of peace and comfort compels them to think of their regimental comrades who are still roughing it 'out there.'

Here is one staring through the perfumed smoke of a Turkish weed. 'Look at me with this box of 50' he soliloquises 'and many a bloke in the trenches would give all he'd got for a tab.' When he was first brought in, he was not quite accustomed to the flavour of these Arabian-scented brands. 'Just had an Egyptian Cigarette – nearly suffocated me' he will say after some fair caller has left him his first packet. Then a week later 'You bet we don't smoke common fags here! Folks bring you any amount of the classy stuff, especially if you have been to the front.' The next day perhaps, he has a full box of 'Woodbines' sent by post. What does he do with them. Tell it not in Gath – he palms them off, in place of pennies, to pay for his losses at 'nap.'

This plenitude of tobacco causes the nurses no end of trouble on account of the surreptitious whiffs taken at prohibited times. 'Who is that smoking out of hours?' says a sister, trying to be severe and the answer comes from the guilty one in splints: 'It's the bullets you can smell sister.' He means the little round balls of toffee which she pops into his expectant mouth after a medicine dose. He would complain about any other kind of bullet being put into him now he has come home. He takes nothing seriously. He refuses to be alarmed when the lady with the thermometer exclaims ruefully at his high temperature. He merely runs his finger along the line of the chart and says 'Like a switchback, ain't it?'

Once every Wednesday and Saturday, on visiting days, a little army of barbers comes to the college and distributes itself about the wards. Looking more like a canvasser for a brand new tea, a tonsor, carrying a small Gladstone bag, puts his head through the folding door and calls out 'Anybody for shaves or haircuts here?' Likely as not there is a chorus of replies 'Over here Dad.' Those who are 'all right on their pins' take a seat near the medicine table in the centre of the room and the clip-clip of the scissors intermingles with the chatter of the visitors and the rustle of paper wrappers as parcels containing grapes, bananas, cigarettes and jam are being unfolded on the beds of the patients by thoughtful mothers, wives, sisters and sweethearts.

At last the barber comes to a hero of the front who has been shot through both legs. He is about to apply the lather when the occupant of the bed remarks 'Hold on a bit Jack! Let me get my harp.' 'Harp?' queries the knight of the razor. 'Here we are' is the reply, as one of those wire-cage arrangements is produced which enables one to sit up comfortably. The applicant for the shave has been in pain, but he does not say so. It is the Tommy Atkins way.

'Spring to attention, boys!' sings out the same phlegmatic soldier as the hairdresser is about to retire with this tackle. Then he cogitates 'I had a closer shave than that a fortnight ago. It's just two weeks since I got it.' He does not allow himself to ruminate for long however. He reaches out for the mouth organ which lies on his locker and announces to the ward that he is about to play the instrument between his knees, just to show there is nothing the matter with his legs. He fails miserably poor fellow and the warning finger of the watching 'sister' deters him from further efforts. He then proceeds in the orthodox fashion to render the 'Marseillaise' with his free hands.

There is a little party hobbling down the drive which calls itself 'the crutch platoon.' If he would only admit it every man has a nightmare which he would like to forget. They all know what the others have gone through and have still to suffer. 'Left-right-left-right; pick up your dressing there,' commands a Yeomanry N.C.O. who himself is incapacitated and make a rag-time step with his temporary wooden leg. He will never mount a horse again. How can he be frivolous? It is the Tommy Atkins way.

A special military surgical hospital with 425 beds was established as a section of the 1st Northern General Hospital and much valuable work was done there. Tens of thousands of returned wounded were given care and convalescence in the war hospitals of Tyneside and Northumberland. At the end of the war the hospitals gradually closed down as the last convalescent soldiers were discharged or transferred to other facilities – the last soldier vacated the Northumberland War Hospital over a year after the Armistice on 6 December 1919. Some of the soldiers with complex medical or mental problems were transferred to long-term institutions and would die in them years later, forgotten casualties of the First World War. Others, despite returning to their families, never fully recovered from their exposure to poison gas or injuries they suffered during the war. They endured pain or a wheezing, hacking cough for the rest of their lives, lives so often sadly shortened, and many a mam or grandma would have to say to future generations who would ask where was Dad or Grandad or Uncle so-and–so? 'He died before his time…'

Convalescent soldiers in the 'Hospital Blue' uniforms at the Northumberland War Hospital, 1916.

Communities in Mourning

For others the news came home that their loved one had been killed. In the days and weeks after the first day on the Somme, the 'harvest of death' as one newspaper called it, was displayed by page after page of portraits of local lads killed, injured and missing in action. The impact on communities such as Cramlington, Blyth and Cowpen, where together they lost over 100 local lads on that one 'Black Saturday' of 1 July 1916, was heartbreaking and of course there would be more agonies to come as the battle rolled on into November 1916 and continued to claim its bloody toll. Losses were made all the harder because the boys were being buried hundreds of miles from home or had been posted missing presumed dead. Even though there were frequent special services held to remember all the local lads that had fallen, there was not the closure families so desperately needed, so there were memorial services held in churches and chapels so that families and friends could come together to remember and mourn the passing of the soldier special to them, be he son, father, brother, cousin or marra.

The memorial service for twenty-five-year-old Pte Andrew Easton of 2nd Battalion, Tyneside Scottish, held at the Beaconsfield Primitive Methodist Church on Sunday 23 July 1916 was typical of those special commemorations. Conducted by Revd Peter McPhail in the presence of Pte Easton's parents, William and Agnes Easton of Coburg Street, and a large congregation, the account in the *Blyth News and Wansbeck Chronicle* movingly records:

Letters were read from Pte M. Wilson who was with him 15 minutes before he was hit and from his uncle testifying to his most excellent character. A Bible given to him by his mother on

Pte Edward Gamblin, 9th Battalion, Durham Light Infantry (T.F.), son of Sidney and Elizabeth Gamblin of Gateshead who died of wounds he received in action on 22 August 1915, aged twenty-one. He is buried in the Etaples Military Cemetery, France.

entering the army was handed to a lad with his dying hands to be returned to his parents. The book was covered with trench mud showing it had been well read. He was closely connected with the Sunday Schools and church and was a decided Christian. He joined the Tyneside Scottish for the period of the war and had fallen a pure, brave lad.

Pte Easton's body has never been recovered and his name is carved with many more of his comrades on Thiepval Memorial to the Missing, Somme, France.

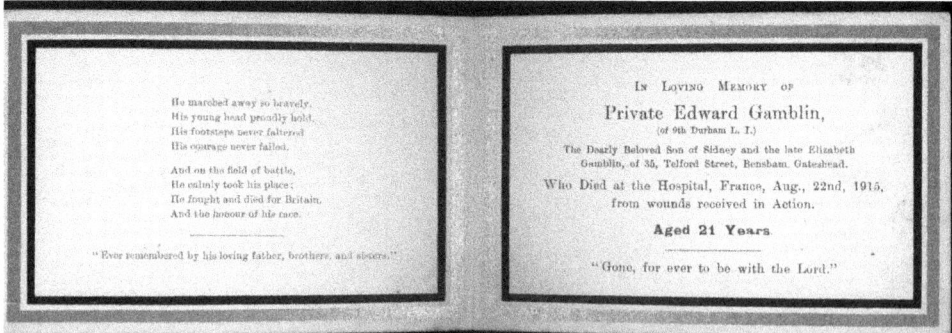

Memorial card for Pte Edward Gamblin

7

MUD, BLOOD AND THE ARMISTICE

As the battles on the Somme rolled on through the latter months of 1916, more and more battalions of the Northumberland Fusiliers were engaged on the front. Among them was 1/4th Battalion, Northumberland Fusiliers (T.F.), who brought with them their mascot, a six-year-old Border terrier cross named Sammy. The little dog had become a well-loved 'character' ever since he first came along to training sessions in Hexham with L/Cpl George Urwin, the man who had raised him from a pup. Sammy went with the battalion to France and proved his worth many times, barking to warn of approaching enemy raiders at night or his sensitive nose serving him well as he raised the alarm if poison gas was around. The little dog was wounded and suffered being gassed during the Second Battle of Ypres. On the Somme, so the story goes, he was blown up by a 'Jack Johnson' shell but by some miracle landed on

The battalion drum major and Sammy, the Border terrier cross mascot of 1/4th Battalion, Northumberland Fusiliers (T.F.), 1916.

his feet without a scratch. Tragically, the end came when Sammy was accidentally blown up during field firing practice at Warfusee in Belgium. His little body was recovered from the field and sent back to a British taxidermist and Sammy stood in a glass case at the Drill Hall in Hencotes for many years. Today he greets visitors as they arrive at the Fusiliers Museum of Northumberland in the Abbot's Tower, Alnwick Castle.

The war just seemed to drag on, taking a horrific toll on the men and those who had survived years of it were getting weary. The 19th (Service) Battalion, Northumberland Fusiliers (Pioneers), notes published in *St George's Gazette* captures the atmosphere of leaving the front line, even if it was just for a while:

B.E.F. 23 August 1916

Dusty, parched, sweating with the heat of August, the column winds steadily along the road. All are afoot and the Battalion, weary of the ceaseless work, seeks rest. The Station is well behind and the road winds uphill. Ripples of the sultry air in crimson flood, surge and billow over the fields; blue cornflowers bob and straggle like flotsam. Away over the path, partridges scurry and but for the rhythmic beat of the feet, the jingling of equipment and the hum of conversation – well accustomed sounds – all is silent. Not the whirr of the aeroplanes, not the infernal rattle of the machine guns, not the booming of the guns or the screech of the shells, not the chatter and moan of the 75s – only peace.

Working as a team, good comradeship or working 'buddy-buddy' are all terms known only too well to soldiers over the last 100 years. Here are soldiers of 5th Battalion, Northumberland Fusiliers (T.F.), cleaning clothes and equipment after their return from the attack on Le Sars, Toutencourt, in October 1916.

Long was the trek and hot. The amazing stillness, the ever-changing views cast a spell and men marched onward. Villages were whole; no hideous battered ruins offended the eye, spires proudly overtopped the clustering trees. Such trees, full leaved, gorgeous, umbrageous! Memories of gaunt, splintered, shattered trunks faded with all their tragic associations, all their appalling reek. Sweetness of crops passing to ripeness had succeeded the foulness of war passing to decay.

Onwards to billets in a secluded village! Undulating ground, rolling plains, eminences crowned with copses, fields of yellowing corn, a winding, sparkling stream flowing amidst a glorious woodland, such was the environment. Day faded to dusk and dusk to night through all the wonders of a perfect sunset. No slow mounting, rolling fateful banks of cloud sprang up from the earth to mar the serenity of the scene and dusty, tired soldiers lay shrouded in the silence.

It was a dream. The dream lasted five days. Then back into it again – bivouacs and work. A light railway runs alongside the camp and a puffing engine pulls a solitary coach, apparently aimlessly. The men have christened it the 'leave train'. It is always *empty!*'

Two Victoria Crosses for the Tyneside Irish on the First Day of Arras

The Victoria Cross is our nation's highest award for gallantry and recognises acts of supreme valour in battle. Awards of the VC are rare, so to see two awarded on the same day in the same action to men serving in battalions of the Tyneside Irish Brigade really is a remarkable occurrence and reflects the critical situation these men were facing.

After the horrific losses during the Battle of the Somme between July and November 1916 and with the introduction of conscription in early 1916, the character of locally raised units changed dramatically. Although many local men did still serve with their own county regiments, many of the drafts of soldiers who came to replace the fallen included men from all over Great Britain. If your old battalion or battalions of your

Left: Pte Ernest Sykes VC, 27th (Service) Battalion, Northumberland Fusiliers (4th Tyneside Irish).

Right: Lt-Cpl Tom Bryan VC 25th (Service) Battalion, Northumberland Fusiliers (2nd Tyneside Irish).

regiment were up to capacity, if you were a trained man or a soldier recuperated after wounds or sickness and returned to the front, you would be sent to join the regiment that had the most immediate need of reinforcements. This, however, did not mean the men were lacking when it came down to fighting – far from it, as exemplified during the first day of the Battle of Arras, France. It was Easter Monday 9 April 1917 and the Tyneside Irish Brigade were in the thick of the advance.

Pte Ernest Sykes (thirty-two) was a Mossley-born Yorkshireman, a father of three who had worked as a platelayer at the London & North Western Railway before the war. Sykes was serving in the 27th (Service) Battalion, Northumberland Fusiliers (4th Tyneside Irish), when his battalion was held up by intense fire from front and flank and was suffering heavy casualties. Pte Sykes, who had himself been wounded earlier in the war, went out under this heavy fire with complete disregard for his own safety and went forward to help his wounded comrades, an act recorded in the citation for his Victoria Cross:

For most conspicuous bravery and devotion to duty when his battalion in attack was held up about 350 yards in advance of our lines by intense fire from front and flank, and suffered heavy casualties. Pte Sykes, despite this heavy fire, went forward and brought back four wounded—he made a fifth journey and remained out under conditions which appeared to be certain death, until he had bandaged all those who were too badly wounded to be moved. These gallant actions, performed under incessant machine gun and rifle fire, showed an utter contempt of danger.

L/Cpl Tom Bryan (thirty-five) had been born in Worcestershire but moved to Castleford, Yorkshire, when he was a young lad – he grew up there and had worked at the Whitwood Colliery before the war. A good strong man, he was a well-known player for Castleford Northern Rugby Union, and he was also a married man with a family of four children. On 9 April 1917 Bryan was serving in 25th (Service) Battalion (2nd Tyneside Irish), Northumberland Fusiliers. While recuperating from his wound in hospital at Alnwick, he related this account of his gallant actions:

On this great day our lads were held up by a machine gun, which was so well hidden that we couldn't check its deadly work. I therefore made up my mind to put a stop to its activities, so creeping over the top, I went from shell hole to shell hole in 'No Man's Land.' I crept into a communication trench, which was held by the enemy, where I came across three Germans. This was at six o'clock in the morning. These men were so surprised that they surrendered without showing any fight and two of them presented me with their watches. I thereupon sent them down to the base with some of my men. I then went forward again, along with Sgt-Maj. Foster and ran across a German officer, who also seemed delighted. Not many minutes afterwards I surprised another Hun, who gave up his arms as meekly as a lamb. An hour later I was still prowling around, trying to fix the German machine gun team but was unable to spot it. While working my way along, I was spotted by one of the enemy, who, letting drive, caught me in the right arm.

Following this bit of hard luck I decided to try rapid fire on the place where I thought the machine gun was placed and on this being carried out, we found to our glee that the gun that had been spitting forth its fire of death barked no more. Two of the gun team tried to get away under our rapid fire, but I shot both of them.

I stayed with my comrades until half-past one mid-day, after which I left to have my wound dressed. With the machine gun and its gunners destroyed, it was now an easy matter for our boys to advance.

Bryan's actions took out a machine gun that had proved a danger to the success of the advance and, if had not been the gallantry of Tom Bryan, it could well have taken the lives of many more. Both VC heroes Sykes and Bryan were later honoured with civic events in both their home towns and in Newcastle.

By the closing months of 1917, as British forces faced another bitterly cold winter on the Western Front, there was some hope that the conflict was turning in favour of the allies. A West Tyne officer, in a letter to his father in October 1917, wrote:

We have now reached the stage when we have a superiority in artillery of all calibres, and no trench system can stand against the bombardments we can put up when we desire. He, of course, clings to his deep dug-outs for protection, where the ground is suitable, but in this sector, where the ground is flat and the soil wet and heavy, and the trench system consisted of breastworks laboriously constructed, he has been forced to adopt other methods, when our advance rendered his previous system of breastworks untenable. So he evolved the shell-hole-pill-box method of defence, where every farmhouse is strengthened by concrete into a miniature fort, the intervening ground being held by detached parties of men and machine guns, and the existing shell holes used for cover.

The exact position of the front line is thus somewhat confused and uncertain, and small relieving and rationing parties are often walking into the opposing lines in the darkness, sometimes getting away in the resulting confusion and sometimes getting captured. The ground in the forward area is rapidly assuming the same hopeless type of wilderness look as was seen on the Somme last year.

The terrific bombardments and barrages soon churn up every yard of ground, shatter nearly all the trees, and level villages to the ground, until all becomes a barren waste. I remember recently guiding one of our officers who had just returned from leave to a village in the forward area. I landed him right in the centre of what had once been the village street – that of a village of 2,000 or 3,000 inhabitants – and informed him where he was, to his great amazement, as not a single wall was standing, and he was looking for signs of the village in the distance.

Away beyond our front lies the ground still in German possession, the green fields and red-tiled houses, and lines of trees offering a pleasing contrast to the brown waste on our side; and the pity is that that fair picture has to be converted into another brown waste before we can wrest it from its present holders. We have to employ an army of men to repair the roads and railways behind our advance, and erect billets and bivouacs for our men. A network of trench tramways soon springs up behind our lines, this useful and efficient means of transport being used for taking up ammunition, supplies, and working parties, and also for evacuating the wounded. They considerably relieve the pressure on the roads, which at times get fearfully congested, as well as being well defined targets for enemy's artillery.

The weather has been all against us during the recent fighting, and our successes are all the more noteworthy, as to lie out during the cold and rain, and then fight on top of this without a hot meal, takes a good deal of grit as well as physical stamina. The artillery have had quite a rough time in getting forward into new positions over rough ground, their only protection being rolls of camouflage to screen them from observation.

Our own work this time has all been in making the roads passable in the ground we have captured. One gets to the side of an old road and gazes at the ploughed up ground, with no vestige of road visible, and wonders where to begin. A line of stumps of trees often gives the line, and then, on digging down quite passable pieces of the old road are discovered, although at times the shell craters take a lot of filling in and making up.

We have been very fortunate in regard to the lightness of our casualties, as we got shelled every day on our work, and especially after enemy aeroplanes had inspected and reported us to their batteries. Enemy aeroplanes have been very busy, and do a fair amount of bombing in revenge, I suppose, for our efforts in that direction. At night, when they come over, and our searchlights pick them up, they seem like giant silver insects in the sky, but they have a very nasty sting, and I prefer to be shelled any day to having bombs dropped on me. I am still going strong myself, and have not felt the strain of our strenuous times so much as during the last fighting we were in. We are now having a short rest and getting ourselves reconciled to facing another winter out here.

The winter of 1917 rolled into 1918. Germany saw the Americans were coming in force to fight on the Western Front and their only chance of victory over the allies was to launch a spring offensive throwing all they had into it – history remembers it as the *Kaiserschlact*. In *When the Lantern of Hope Burned Low: The story of the 1/4th Northumberland Fusiliers T.F. during the German Offensives of March, April, May 1918* R. Wilfrid Callin recounted how fatigue and war weariness affected the men:

Apart from heavy casualties, the worst feature of the Somme fighting retreat (of 1918) was undoubtedly the incredible fatigue and lack of sleep. Men simply could not keep awake despite the danger and the slightest respite found them in deep slumber. Any bed was a good bed – a

Cadre of recuperated soldiers ready to return to front line service with the Northumberland Fusiliers *c.* 1917. The wound stripes worn on the left forearm by many in the photo tell the story that some of these lads had been wounded as many as three times before.

heap of stones by the roadside, a ditch, an open field, a sloping bank. Cold and hunger were forgotten in nature's overwhelming clamour for sleep. Passing through Moreuil on the eve of Good Friday, men dropped asleep on doorsteps for three or four minutes at a time, walked a few yards further, slept on another doorstep and so on…Physically the men had come to the very end of their tether and only will power kept them going.

Despite the fatigue, despite the demoralising effect a retreat was bound to have, this back fortnight was illuminated by instances of individual bravery worthy of the highest traditions of the Fifth Fusiliers and the British Army; whilst the set teeth and bulldog tenacity of the battalion as a unit, contesting each mile of ground, holding on to the last moment, counter attacking when hopelessly outnumbered, robbed the enemy of his vital elan, made him hesitate when hesitation meant failure and contributed a full quota to the fighting which robbed him of the prize for which he strove so much.

Battalions of the Northumberland Fusiliers were in action to the very end and Capt. C. H. Cooke recorded that moment in *Historical Records of the 9th (Service) Battalion Northumberland Fusiliers*:

The news of the Armistice came through to the men of 9th Battalion via a communiqué from 61st Division headquarters at 08.00 hours stating 'Hostilities will cease 1100 hours to-day November 11th. Stand fast on line reached at that hour which will be reported by wire to Corps Headquarters. Defensive precautions will be maintained. There will be no intercourse of any description with the enemy. Ends.'

The men cheered and Lieutenant-Colonel Thomson spoke to the companies in turn, telling them to keep up the training. The Brigadier arrived and addresses the men in similar terms. Training then proceeded! Such was the reception of the news by a hard-fighting battalion, with all its honours fresh upon it. What a contrast to the wild scenes at home. It really took time for the significance of Armistice to be appreciated. No more shells, no more rifle-fire, no more gas, no more machine-guns, no more over-the-top, no more ------ oh! All these things were finished. After more than three years of it, the 'old hands' could scarcely realize the position. Immense silence followed the continual inferno of flame and noise. Eyes still shone with the strange light of perplexity, that far-away look of men who went through life expecting each moment to meet death. The everlasting nearness of the borderland, the feeling of it's almost inevitability left their mark on the strained features. It is still there for thoughtful people to see – the mark that proclaims a Man.

Lt-Col. W. A. Vignoles DSO., officers and senior NCOs, 9th (Service) Battalion, Northumberland Fusiliers, Bournonville, France, May 1918. (Fusiliers Museum of Northumberland)

8

GOODBYE TO ALL THAT

Over the weeks and months after the Armistice began the slow process of demobilizing the men of the armed forces began. It was a time of final reckoning as the prisoner of war camps were emptied of British personnel, the military hospitals closed one by one, and the final 'presumed dead' notifications of death were issued by the War Office to the next of kin of those who had been posted 'missing in action' – some of their families never accepted the decision and held out hope that their dear father, brother, son or husband would return one day. For most the decision was accepted and the war memorials to the fallen were erected across Tyneside.

It is true to say that everybody on Tyneside lost a family member or knew someone as a friend or neighbour who did not return from the First World War. The Northumberland Fusiliers earned sixty-seven battle honours and five Victoria Crosses but at a cost of 16,000 dead during the conflict. Add to that the local men serving in a host of other corps and regiments, Royal Navy and Air Force, and the death toll on Tyneside meant that everywhere lost someone. Even Meldon, claimed as one of the fifty-one 'Thankful Villages' that had all its men who went to war return, had Cpl George Alder Eamens, a son of the village who had emigrated before the war, killed in action in France while serving in 53rd Battalion, Australian Infantry Force. The impact of such losses, especially on rural communities, was profound and talk of 'the Loss of a Generation' became common parlance in the north-east.

For those who did return there was the warm welcome home and the celebrations of Peace Day, but soon after the bitter bite of unemployment followed, as did the realisation that after all they had done, the country they had fought for fell a long way short of the promised 'Land Fit for Heroes'. Many of those with disabilities as a result of their military service had to fight yet again to get the benefits they needed and deserved. Tragically some of them died before they received them. However, their old pals did not desert them and soon there were all manner of associations

Some of the ladies of Byker in their Sunday best clothes and fancy dress at their Victory Tea Party, 1919. A banner for the returned servicemen hung over the street read – 'We're Proud of You.'

Children's street party at Wallsend to celebrate victory, 1919. There are some smiles but there are also some sad little faces too of children who knew their daddies would not be coming home from the war.

including Comrades of the Great War, British Legion and those for Army divisions, battalions and regiments set up to keep those links forged in war and to do their best to help those lads or their families if they fell on hard times.

It was at one of the earliest reunion dinners for men of 17th (Service) Battalion, Northumberland Fusiliers (N.E.R. Pioneers), held on 13 September 1919 that Sir Alexander Kaye Butterworth, General Manager of the N.E.R. (whose only son, the notable composer Lt George Butterworth MC, had been killed in action on the Somme while serving in 13th Battalion, Durham Light Infantry) delivered the following address:

Now you are back – North Eastern Railwaymen, the same as before. The same and yet I fancy *not* quite the same. I cannot think that anyone who has been through what you have been through; seen what you have seen, achieved what you have achieved can ever be exactly what he was before it all happened.

You must have learned much since you left Salisbury Plain in November 1915 and it will be for you to teach us whom you left behind something of the lessons you have learned. Something of the meaning of comradeship and the meaning of self-sacrifice, of discipline in its highest and best sense and the secret, hardly to be learned it would seem, except in the strain and stress of the fighting line, of how to keep smiling when things look blackest.

Never has the old country which we all love and which you fought for been in greater need of wise guidance and devoted service but though, as I fear, we have difficult days before us, if Englishmen serve their country in the days of peace as bravely and unselfishly as her soldiers have done during the last 5 years, I for one have no fear about the issue.

The lads of the north did indeed pull together and communities did pull through but things were never quite the same again. This poignant poem, published in *St George's Gazette* in August 1917, captures so much of Remembrance a century ago and evokes a torch of Remembrance that has now passed to us who come after the last of them:

OUR ROLL OF HONOUR

We stand one with the men who died,
Come dawn, come dark, we have these beside
Living or dead we are comrades all,
Our battles are won by the men that fall.

He who died quick with his face to the foe,
In the heart of a friend must needs die slow;
Over his grave shall be heard the call,
The battle is won by the men that fall.

For a dead man leaves you work to do,
Your heart's so full that you fight for two;
And the dead man's aim is the best of all,
The battle is won by the men that fall.

O lads, dear lads, who were loyal and true,
The worst of the fight was borne by you;
So the word shall go to cottage and hall,
Our battles are won by the men that fall.

When peace dawns over the countryside,
Our thanks shall be to the lads that died,
O quiet hearts, can you hear us tell
How peace was won by the men that fell?

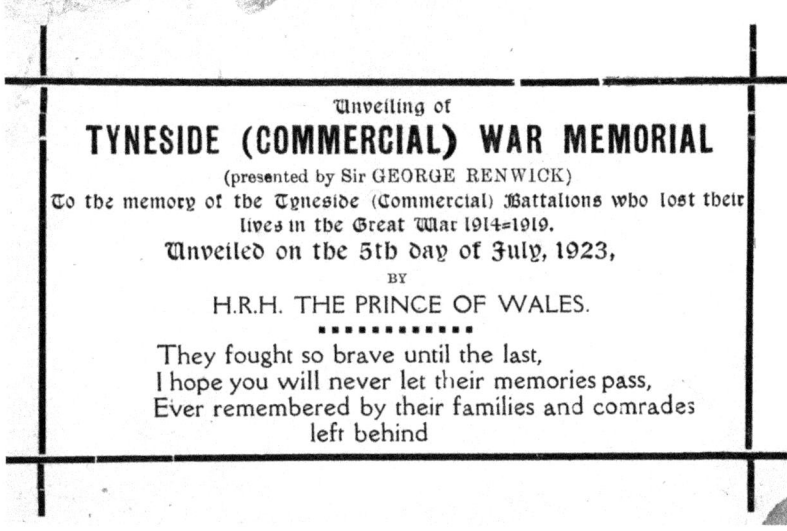

Unveiling of
TYNESIDE (COMMERCIAL) WAR MEMORIAL
(presented by Sir GEORGE RENWICK)
To the memory of the Tyneside (Commercial) Battalions who lost their lives in the Great War 1914=1919.
Unveiled on the 5th day of July, 1923,
BY
H.R.H. THE PRINCE OF WALES.
• • • • • • • • • • • •
They fought so brave until the last,
I hope you will never let their memories pass,
Ever remembered by their families and comrades left behind

A simple commemoration card for the opening of the Commercials Memorial, unveiled by the Prince of Wales on his visit to Newcastle on 5 July 1923.

COMMERCIAL BATTALIONS' WAR MEMORIAL, NEWCASTLE.

The Commercials Monument entitled *The Response* erected to commemorate the raising of B Company, 9th Battalion, and the 16th, 18th and 19th (Service) Battalions, Northumberland Fusiliers, by the Newcastle & Gateshead Chamber of Commerce.

The Newcastle War Memorial in Old Eldon Square, unveiled by Field Marshall Sir Douglas Haig in 1923.

Memorial to the fallen of the 6th (Newcastle) Battalion, Northumberland Fusiliers (T.F.), erected next to the west end of St Thomas's Church, Barras Bridge, Newcastle, pictured shortly after its unveiling in 1924.

BIBLIOGRAPHY

Armstrong, Craig, *Newcastle upon Tyne in the Great War* (Barnsley, 2015)

Brewis, Alfred, *The Northumberland Fusiliers (The Fighting Fifth)*, (Newcastle, 1915)

Broderick-Thompson, Captain A. (ed.), *The War Record of Old Dunelmians 1914–1919* (Sunderland, 1919)

Buckley, Captain Francis, *Q.6.A and other places. Recollections of 1916, 1917, 1918* (London, 1920)

Buckley, Captain Francis (ed.), *War History of the 7th Northumberland Fusiliers* (Newcastle, 1919)

Callin, Revd R. Wilfrid, *When the Lantern of Hope Burned Low: The story of the 1/4th Northumberland Fusiliers T.F. during the German Offensives of March, April, May 1918.* (Hexham, n.d.)

Cantlie, James, *First Aid to the Injured* (London, 1915)

Cook, Marriott, Sir, Bond Hubert, C., *History of the Asylum War Hospitals in England and Wales* (HMSO, 1920)

Cooke, Capt. C. H., *Historical Records of the 9th (Service) Battalion Northumberland Fusiliers* (Newcastle 1928)

Cooke, Capt. C. H. *Historical Records of the 16th (Service) Battalion Northumberland Fusiliers* (Newcastle 1923)

Cooke, Capt. C. H. *Historical Records of the 19th (Service) Battalion Northumberland Fusiliers* (Newcastle, 1920)

Gladden, Norman, *The Somme 1916: A Personal Account* (London, 1974)

Hurrell, George, and Harland, George P., *The History of Newcastle General Hospital* (Newcastle, 1966)

Johnson, Ian, *Newcastle Commercials* (revised addition, Newcastle, 2016)

Lavery, Felix (comp.) Keating, Joseph and O'Connor, T. P., *Irish Heroes in the War* (London, 1917)

Liddle, Peter, *The Soldier's War 1914–1918* (London, 1988)

Middlebrook, Martin *The First Day on the Somme* (London 1971)

Peacock, Basil, *The Royal Northumberland Fusiliers* (London, 1970)

Peacock, Basil, *Tinker's Mufti: An Autobiography* (London, 1974)

Reader, W. J., *At Duty's Call: A Study in Obsolete Patriotism* (Manchester, 1988)

Sandilands, Brig. H. R., *Fifth in the Great War: A History of the 1st and 2nd Northumberland Fusiliers, 1914–1918* (Dover, 1938)

Sellwood, A. V., *The Saturday Night Soldiers* (London, 1966)

Shakespear, Lt-Col. John, *Historical Records of the 17th (Service) Battalion Northumberland Fusiliers (N.E.R. Pioneers)*, (Newcastle, 1926)

Shakespear, Lt-Col. John, *Historical Records of the 18th (Service) Battalion Northumberland Fusiliers (Pioneers)*, (Newcastle, 1920)

Sheen, John, *Tyneside Irish 24th, 25th & 26th & 27th (Service) Battalions of the Northumberland Fusiliers* (Barnsley, 1998)

Simkins, Peter, *Kitchener's Army: The Raising of the New Armies 1914–1916* (Barnsley, 2007)

Stewart, Graham, and Sheen, John, *Tyneside Scottish: 20th, 21st, 22nd and 23rd (Service) Battalions of the Northumberland Fusiliers* (Barnsley, 1998)

Storey, Neil, and Kay, Fiona, *Newcastle Battalions in Action on the Somme* (Tyne Bridge, 2016)

Storey, Neil, *The Tommy's Handbook* (Stroud, 2014)

Storey, Neil R., *Women in the First World War* (Shire, 2010)

Storey, Neil, *Zeppelin Blitz* (Stroud, 2015)

Ternan, Brig-Gen. Trevor, *The Story of the Tyneside Scottish* (Newcastle, 1919)

Westlake, Ray, *British Battalions on the Somme* (Barnsley, 1994)

Westlake, Ray, *Kitcheners Army* (Tunbridge Wells, 1989)

Westlake, Ray, *The Territorial Battalions* (London, 1986)

Reference Books and Official Publications

Annual Report of the State of the Royal Victoria Infirmary for the Sick and Lame Poor (Newcastle, annually 1914–1918)

British Red Cross Society & Order of St John of Jerusalem, *Final Reports by the Joint War Committee and the Joint War Finance Committee of the British Red Cross Society and Order of St John of Jerusalem in England on Voluntary Aid Rendered to the Sick and Wounded at Home and Abroad and to British Prisoners of War 1914–19* (HMSO, 1921)

Final Report and Balance Sheets of the Elswick and Scotswood Workers' War Relief Fund (Newcastle, 1920)

Kelly's Directory of Durham and Northumberland (London, 1914)

Soldiers Died in the Great War: Northumberland Fusiliers (HMSO, 1921)

St. Mary Magdelene Home for Incurables Annual Reports (Newcastle, annually 1914–1918)

War Office, *Scheme for the Organisation of Voluntary Aid in England and Wales* (HMSO, 1909)

Newspapers, Journals and Magazines

Alnwick & County Gazette
Berwick Advertiser
Blyth News and Wansbeck Telegraph
Evening Chronicle (Newcastle)
Family Tree Magazine
Hexham Courant
Illustrated Chronicle (Newcastle)
Illustrated War News
Morpeth Herald
St. Georges Gazette
The Colliery Guardian
The Evening Chronicle
The Growler
The Newcastle Daily Journal
The North Mail
The Northerner
The Quaysider
The Rutherfordian
The Shipbuilder
The Times
War Illustrated

ACKNOWLEDGEMENTS

Neil Storey and Fiona Kay would like to thank: Newcastle Library; Lesley Freyter, Fusiliers Museum of Northumberland; Maj. Charles Whiteley, 101 Regiment, Royal Artillery; Capt. 'Jack' Frost, 204 (Tuneside Scottish) Battery, Royal Artillery; Maj. Chester Potts T.D., Chairman of the Northumberland and North East Fusiliers Association; Keith Laws, Chairman Northumberland Royal British Legion; Dean Christopher Dallison and Kate Sussams at St Nicholas Cathedral, Newcastle; Alan Fidler, Northumbria World War One Commemoration Project; Bill Corcoran, Tyneside Irish Brigade Association; Billy Embleton, Jim Smith and Ian Johnson for their kind support, encouragement and help with this book. Most of the images in this book are drawn from the authors' collections, unless otherwise stated. Every attempt has been made to seek permission for copyright material used in this book. However, if we have inadvertently used copyright material without permission/acknowledgement, we apologise and we will make the necessary correction at the first opportunity.